One Last String to Cut

RICHARD BRYSON

ISBN 979-8-89112-865-1 (Paperback)
ISBN 979-8-89112-866-8 (Digital)

Copyright © 2024 Richard Bryson
All rights reserved
First Edition

All rights reserved. No part of this publication may be reproduced, distributed, or transmitted in any form or by any means, including photocopying, recording, or other electronic or mechanical methods without the prior written permission of the publisher. For permission requests, solicit the publisher via the address below.

Covenant Books
11661 Hwy 707
Murrells Inlet, SC 29576
www.covenantbooks.com

CONTENTS

Introduction v
Chapter 1: Not a Good Start 1
Chapter 2: Musical Jobs 27
Chapter 3: Psych 48
Chapter 4: Off to the School of Prison 76
Chapter 5: Free Man Again? 120

INTRODUCTION

I'M WRITING THIS BOOK FOR two reasons. My first reason is to glorify my Savior and Lord Jesus Christ. This book is my testimony of what he's done in my life. My testimony of what he's healed me of, what he delivered me from. This is my testimony of how he changed me from a homicidal, suicidal, and "want to be a serial killer" into a mature man of God.

My second reason for this book is to help other people who are going through or have gone through the same things I did. To show people the wrong way to deal with their problems (the way I did in the past) and the right way to deal with their problems (the way I am now).

Don't get me wrong, this is not a self-help book. I'm just an ordinary man from whom, hopefully, you can learn. The best way to learn in this life is from other people's good and bad choices. So please, learn from the good and bad choices that

I made. That way, you won't have to go down the same destructive path I went down.

My hope is that the Lord will work through this book to show those people who are hurting, who are bound up, who are on the edge of giving up, and who have lost all hope to show them that there is someone willing, able, and ready to help them, to comfort them, to free them, and to give them hope. His name is Jesus Christ. He helped me; I know he can help you, too, if you want his help.

Let me ask you a question. Are you tired of waking up every morning tired of life, depressed, angry, bitter, confused, fearful, hopeless? Have you tried one option after another, trying to find peace, hope, comfort, closure, freedom, or whatever you're looking for? How did it work out for you? Did you find what you're looking for?

If it didn't work out for you and you're still looking for better options, look to Jesus. I know from personal experience that he is the only person who can and will be everything you need him to be in your life. You tried everything else. What do you have to lose? NOTHING! You have nothing to lose and everything to gain.

CHAPTER 1

Not a Good Start

LET ME INTRODUCE MYSELF. My name is Richard Paul Bryson Jr. I was born on March 15, 1964, in Pittsburgh, Pennsylvania.

I know that some people are saying to themselves, "Richard, who? I've never heard of him. Who is he?"

That's a legitimate question. I'm not famous. The world doesn't know my name. I'm just an ordinary, average man who's been on the path of death and destruction for most of my life.

I'm just a man who can understand and relate to the hurt and pain, to the anger, frustration, resentment, confusion, fear, regret, and hopelessness that way too many people are going through and are feeling right now.

I'm just a man who knows what it's like to be picked on, bullied, laughed at, mocked, and ridiculed. I know what it's like to be an outcast, to be rejected. I know what it's like to feel murderous hatred toward certain people. I can understand and relate to being shamed and embarrassed in front of my peers. I know the feeling of hopelessness. I know what it's like to live twenty-four hours a day thinking about death.

I was a man who was hateful, vengeful, unforgiving, and hopeless. A man who didn't care about anything or anyone, including myself: I wanted to die and take as many people with me as I could.

But now, through Jesus, I'm a man who loves and cares about everyone. I want to see good things happen to everybody. I can now forgive people who do wrong to me instead of wanting to kill them.

My dad's name was Richard. He died in a car crash when I was four years old. I never really knew anything about him, what he liked, what he did. But my life went on.

Had my dad not died in that car crash when I was four years old, my life may have turned out to be a lot different than it was. Maybe it would have, maybe it wouldn't have. One can only wonder.

My mom's name is Nancy. She's a retired Mixologist. A mixologist is a bartender who went to school to learn the proper ways to work behind a bar.

She was very good at her job. She could mix any drink that a customer wanted.

My sister's name is Kim. She's two years older than me. She's a very skilled Paralegal who lives in Michigan.

I had a younger brother whose name was Jeff. He was a year younger than me. He died in June of 2015. He committed suicide, killing himself with a gun.

After my dad died, my mom did the best she could raising us. But with three young kids, it wasn't easy for her. There wasn't any manual on the proper way to raise children. So basically, she was winging it. She was doing the best that she knew how to do.

Another thing that didn't make it easy for her was me. I was born with a heart problem.

When I was born, the doctors found something wrong with my heart. What they found was a clogged artery. One of my arteries, either going to or coming from my heart, was too narrow for the blood to properly go through it.

For some reason, the doctors couldn't operate on me at birth. So in 1969, when I was five years old, the doctors at Children's Hospital of Pittsburgh performed my first heart surgery. However, something happened with my heart that in 1971, when I was seven years old, they had to do the same operation again. That second operation finally fixed whatever the problem was with my heart.

After the surgeries, I would occasionally get chest pains. I went to the doctor about it. They checked me out and said I was alright. Their diagnosis for my chest pain was scar tissue. They must have been right because there has never been a third heart surgery.

During my stay in the hospital for my surgeries, I wasn't scared or nervous. As a matter of fact, I wasn't feeling any negative feelings at all. Maybe it's because I was too young to realize the severity of the situation.

I don't know how my family was feeling at that time. I don't know if they were feeling scared, angry, nervous, or concerned, or if they were feeling anything at all. It was something I never talked about with them.

When I was growing up, I was different from my family, not only physically with my heart problem but also with character traits.

My family were bold go-getters, knowing what they wanted—going after what they wanted. On the other hand, I was timid and reserved, not knowing what I wanted. They were confident in themselves. I had no confidence in myself. They were outgoing. I was an introvert. They saw a bright future for themselves. I saw a bleak future for myself.

I don't know if I had the same character traits in me that they had in them. But one thing I do know. If I did have the same character traits that they did, I either hid them, or didn't know they were there, or just didn't bring them out to use them.

But God made me different from birth. Different from my family. And different from my friends and neighbors.

Did you know that being different is a blessing in disguise? For most of my life, I didn't feel this way. I thought of being different as a curse, as something to be ashamed of. But I was looking at it from the wrong perspective. I was looking at it from a negative perspective instead of a positive one.

Think about it. There are advantages to being different from the crowd. One major advantage is you know who your real friends are. Your real friends will stick with you, will stick up for you. Your false friends won't.

While you're being different from the crowd, acting differently, speaking differently, and thinking differently, your false friends will slowly but surely start separating themselves from you. They'll stop hanging around you for whatever reason they come up with.

Another major advantage of being different is you can be yourself. You don't have to be what the people you hang around want you to be.

I want you to realize something. There has never been, and there will never be, a person like you. God made you different, unique, a true one-of-a-kind.

Do you know what happens when you try to fit in with the crowd? You're lying to yourself and to them. You're trying to be someone that you're not meant to be. You're becoming trapped in a situation that you don't want to be in or shouldn't be in.

If you be yourself and be who God made you to be, eventually, you'll find the crowd that you belong in. The crowd that's going to accept you for who you are, not who they want you to be.

Did you know that a lot of times, God chooses people who are different from the crowd? He chooses the outcasts, the people that society rejects.

For example, look at the first twelve disciples that Jesus chose. Four were fishermen, one was a tax collector, and one was a traitor. Half of Jesus' first twelve disciples were outcasts and were different from the crowd.

And what did Jesus do with those disciples? He turned the known world upside down. He worked through those disciples in a mighty, supernatural way, healing people and setting people free from their bondages.

He worked through twelve different men from the crowd to further his kingdom. How? By those disciples making a positive difference in the lives of those around them.

So if you're different from the crowd, if you feel like an outcast, don't be ashamed or embarrassed by it. Don't look at it as a curse like I did. Look at it as a blessing. Embrace it! Be the unique, one-of-a-kind person that God made you to be.

Who knows, God may have called you to be his next different from the crowd disciple that he wants to work through to change the world.

When I was young, I didn't understand the idea of being different as a blessing. I was ashamed and embarrassed by it. I felt like an outcast because of it.

So I did what most kids do. I tried to find a crowd to fit into. But there wasn't any. I wasn't athletic, so I didn't fit in with them. I wasn't smart, so I didn't fit in with them. I wasn't popular, so I didn't fit in with them. I wasn't into drugs, so I didn't fit in with them.

There was no crowd that I fit in with. I was on the outside looking in. I was an island unto myself.

Had I known then what I know now, I could've embraced being different. I could've had a different attitude towards it. But as they say, "Hindsight is twenty-twenty."

However, with the mind frame that I had back then, I was seeing most things through the wrong eyes. I was seeing most things through negative eyes, not positive eyes. I was seeing the bad, not the good.

I started seeing through those wrong eyes early in my life. And, you know what? It eventually became second nature to me. And that hurt me for most of my life.

Looking at the negative instead of the positive, the bad instead of the good, it hurts us and those around us. It's destructive and unproductive. It keeps us blinded to the good things around us. It keeps us from enjoying our lives.

There's a lot of good in this world. There are a lot of good things to see, to do, and to enjoy in this world. If we would just look through positive eyes instead of negative eyes, we would see them and enjoy them.

But it comes down to a personal choice. What eyes do you want to see through, negative, destructive eyes or positive, good eyes?

As I was growing up, I was not a typical kid. I was skinny, shy, very insecure about myself, and a loner. I didn't have a lot of friends.

So when it came time for me to start school, I was not in a good position. And the thing about it is, I didn't even know it.

You know how some kids like school? They look forward to going to school. They want to see their friends. They want to see their favorite teacher. They look forward to the clubs or sports that they are in or want to be in.

I was not one of those kids. School was a mental nightmare for me. Obviously, it didn't start out that way. It happened over time. School became worse and worse for me. Year after year, grade after grade, it became more and more of a mental nightmare for me.

I hated school. I didn't want to go to school. I wanted nothing to do with it. I went to school because I had to go, not because I wanted to go.

Why did I hate school so much? Two words: school bullies! School bullies were a part of my school life. I couldn't get away from them. I couldn't avoid them.

They started on me either in kindergarten or first grade. The teacher asked me to do something in front of the class. When I was finished doing what they asked me to do, a few of the kids in class called me a teacher's pet and laughed at me.

I realize that, on the surface, that's nothing. That's just kids being kids. I'm not denying or disputing that. That's exactly what it was: just kids being kids. It should've gone in one ear and out the other. It should've had no mental effect on me at all.

However, that wasn't the case. With me being shy and very insecure about myself, it hurt. I allowed it to penetrate my mind and my heart.

I was starting to lay the foundation of how I was going to deal with the abuse that was coming my way for the remainder of my school years. I was starting to make the wrong choice in burying my feelings instead of venting them.

And the problem was I didn't even realize I was doing it. I was unknowingly starting to give them power over me. I was allowing them to start to get in my head. And that bad decision I made back then would affect my life and my family's life in a negative, destructive way for years to come.

I remember in elementary school, one of my classmates had me pinned against a fence at school, saying to everyone around, "Where's Richard?" Some of the kids were laughing. I felt ashamed and embarrassed.

The problem is I did nothing to stop it. Again, I kept my feelings to myself instead of venting them.

I could've and should've handled that situation totally differently. I should've stood up for myself verbally or physically. I should've nipped the problem in the bud and shown him and everyone else that I wasn't going to be their verbal and physical punching bag.

That was the perfect time to close the door that I opened to their abuse. But I didn't. I did the exact opposite. I opened the door wide open.

Instead of letting my feelings out like I should have, I buried them. I buried the hurt, pain, anger, shame, embarrassment, and confusion. And do you know what happens when someone buries their negative feelings for too long? They become a walking time bomb. It's not a question of if they'll go off; it's a question of when, where, and who's going to be hurt by it.

I know this from experience. How? Because years after high school, I exploded when I walked into a Fort Myers, Florida, bank and released those buried negative feelings on six innocent bank employees who had nothing to do with my past, who were just doing their jobs.

So there I was in elementary school, not sticking up for myself, not letting my feelings out. I was starting to become a doormat, allowing those school bullies to tread all over me.

I was also, year by year, grade by grade, becoming a walking time bomb. I was on the path of disaster and destruction. And there was no way for me to get off.

I remember when I was in junior high school, there were four or five of my classmates who tied up either a jacket or sweater of mine and passed it around to each other. I felt helpless to do anything about it.

Also, while I was in junior high, I liked a girl whose name was Jeannie. She was around six inches shorter than I was. I told someone that I liked her. I don't know why I told him that I liked her. It was just another bad decision on my part. However, I told him, and the jokes started coming.

They started saying things like, "She's going to need a step ladder to kiss you." Again, I allowed their jokes and laughing at me to penetrate my mind and my heart.

Slowly but surely, I was becoming a prisoner to them. I was slowly but surely getting deeper and deeper into the pit of hopelessness and despair without even knowing it.

By the time I got to high school, I was damaged goods. I was bringing all those negative emotions, all that hurt, pain, embarrassment, shame, humiliation, confusion, anger, and fear that's been building up in me since kinder garden with me.

I was going into high school as a teenager and had lost already. I was going with no hope. I saw no bright future for myself. I was going with a what's the use attitude. I was just going through the motions. I was doing just enough to get by.

Some might ask the question, "If school was that bad for you, why didn't you just quit or drop out?" That's a legitimate question. I didn't quit or drop out of school because it wasn't an option. I was trying to stay off the radar. I was trying to stay unnoticed.

You know how some people like to be in front of a crowd. They like to be the center of attention. They feel comfortable being in the spotlight. I wasn't one of those people. I liked to be off the radar. I liked to be behind the scenes, out of the spotlight.

So if I quit or dropped out of school, I would be putting myself on the radar, in the spotlight, with my classmates in the neighborhood. I would be giving them another opportunity to hurt me. And I was trying to keep those opportunities to a minimum as much as I could.

As much as I hated school, dropping out or quitting school would've been a worse decision than staying in school.

So there I was in school. It was either in junior high or high school. The teacher asked me a question, and I got the answer wrong. Some of the class started laughing and ridiculing me. I felt ashamed and embarrassed.

Again, either in junior high or high school, the teacher called me to do an assignment on the chalkboard in front of the class. I got the answer right, but I wrote it to small on the board. Some of the class couldn't see my answer. So again, they laughed and ridiculed me. I felt embarrassed.

They were mentally destroying me. They were tearing me down day by day, year by year.

When I had to do anything in front of the class, I hated it. Fear overwhelmed me like a tidal wave. Doing anything in front of the class was the worst part of going to school for me.

When we were in high school, during lunch period, we were allowed to go out into the parking lot to smoke, talk, or get some fresh air.

There were many times that I wanted to go out there. But I never did. Why? Because I was afraid of being seen walking across the cafeteria. I was afraid of what people might say, think, or do to me.

I was trapped in my mind. I was a prisoner of my own fear. I allowed those school bullies to have power over me. I gave them control of my mind, of my feelings. I made a really bad decision to actually care about what people thought of me and what they said about me.

I remember one of the bullies that tormented me. His name was Tom. The last thing I heard about him was that one night, during school, he got drunk and passed out on the front porch of his house. While he was passed out, he froze to death.

I never found out if the story was true or not. But one thing was for sure. I never saw him again after that.

Back then, my thinking was, "Good. I'm glad he's dead. That's one less abuser in my life." I didn't shed a tear for him. I didn't lose any sleep over his death.

As a matter of fact, if all my school bullies had died horrific, painful, torturous deaths, I wouldn't have shed a tear. Back then, if they all had died, my thought would've been, "Good riddance. You got what you deserved."

Please, don't get me wrong. I know that a lot of people have gone through or are going through a lot worse abuse than I did.

But, as we all know, everybody is different. Some people are assertive, while other people are passive. Some people have thick skin, while others have thin skin. Some people are mentally strong, while others aren't. Some people are secure in themselves, while other people aren't. Some people are fighters, while other people are not.

I dealt with my school bully situation in the wrong way. I'm not denying that. However, I dealt with it the only way I thought I could.

I'm just glad there weren't any mass school shootings back then. Because if there had been, I may have been one of the ones doing the killing. But that was God's protection. He was looking out for everyone involved.

Looking back on my life, I regret the way I handled a lot of situations, especially the years I went to school.

I'm disappointed with myself for being so passive, thin-skinned, and soft. It's not like I wanted to be. It's not like I made a conscious choice to be that way. I didn't wake up one day and say to myself, "Self, I want to be passive and soft. I want to be a doormat for anyone and everyone to walk all over me."

That's just how I was wired, so to speak. That was just who I was. That was the inner me, the natural way for me to handle negative situations back then.

Let me ask you a question. Take a look at your own lives. Is there at least one bad decision that you've made in your life that you would like to go back and change? Would you like to go back and do it over?

My school years would be one major one for me. However, as we know, we can't go back and change the past.

But there's nothing stopping us from learning from it. How many of those wrong choices that we made in the past have we learned from? How many have we grown from to become better people? How many of those wrong choices can other people learn and grow from?

Outside school, my life was average. After my dad died, my mom got re-married. She married a man named George. He was a truck driver.

They moved my brother, sister, and me to a town called Gibsonia, Pennsylvania. That's a town on the outskirts of Pittsburgh. They found a house on North Pine Circle.

Back then, Gibsonia didn't have a lot of people living in it. It was a spread-out community with lots of space for the kids in the neighborhood to explore and do things.

There was a big field at the end of North Pine Circle. Some of the kids in the neighborhood would sometimes meet up there to do things. Sometimes, we'd play football or baseball there. At other times, we'd play kid games such as kick the can. It was good, clean, fun, and exercise as well.

There was also a big wooded field right next to North Pine Circle that had motorcycle trails in it. Some people really enjoyed riding their motorcycles on those trails.

I drove a motorcycle on those trails a few times. I enjoyed it, but I never felt comfortable driving a motorcycle. Why didn't I feel comfortable? Because I didn't like the idea of getting hurt. I wasn't a big fan of physical pain. I knew that if I was driving a motorcycle, physical pain and I would eventually cross paths. I was trying to avoid that meeting.

My parents moved us to Gibsonia when I was in elementary school. I remember when we moved into our house on North Pine Circle. One of the first people I met there was a kid named John. He and his family were Christians. They weren't just talking about their faith; they were actually living out their faith like they were supposed to do. They were the first genuine Christians that God put in my life.

John and I hit it off quickly. Over time, John would become a real close friend of mine.

But the thing about it is, we were different from each other. He was a Christian, and I wasn't. He was smart, I wasn't. He applied himself, and I was just going through the motions. He was bold and assertive, and I was timid and passive. He was outgoing, and I was shy.

In spite of being different from each other, he never shunned me. He never looked down his nose at me. He never thought he was better than me. He accepted me for who I was and became one of my only friends that I had.

John lived on North Pine Circle. He lived down the street from us. So we hung out together a lot. Both our families had swimming pools. We'd go swimming every once in a while. Sometimes, we'd catch Frisbee together. While other times, we'd shoot basketball in his backyard.

John and I would also have some good, in-depth talks as well. We'd talk about all sorts of stuff—anything from school, jobs, and careers to life and outer space.

Since he was a Christian, the topic of Jesus would also come up in our talks. However, I wasn't ready for Jesus at that time. I wasn't thinking about him, and I wasn't interested in him back then.

One thing I do know is that in spite of my feelings towards Jesus back then, he was ready for me, thinking about me, and interested in me.

Even though I wasn't ready for Jesus back then, John never turned his back on me. He never pushed

Jesus on me. He accepted my decision back then. He did what he was supposed to do. He witnessed to me when he could and lived out his faith.

Outside school, when I was around my family and when I was around John, my life felt "normal."

I remember when I was growing up on North Pine Circle, every once in a while, our family would have family picnics at our house. My Aunts, Uncles, and Cousins would all come over for the day. We'd have burgers, hotdogs, and fresh corn on the cob. We'd go swimming in the pool.

I don't know about the rest of the family, but I had a lot of fun on those particular days. I felt loved and accepted. I felt like I belonged on days like those.

As good as those days were for me, the reality of school was still a part of my life.

School was slowly, day by day, year by year, destroying me. It was destroying my mind. It was destroying my heart. It was destroying any positive future that I might have had.

Those school bullies were tearing me down layer by layer. They broke me. They won, and I lost.

Don't get me wrong. My school life was not an all-day, everyday "Torment Richard" situation. There were a few bearable periods of time in between the torments.

In high school, I actually joined the track and cross-country teams.

One of the abilities that God gave me was the ability to distance run. So it just seemed like the right choice for me to join the track and cross-country teams.

Even though I was on both teams, I never made it to varsity. Why? Because I never gave it my best effort. I gave it a half-hearted effort at best.

I don't know why I joined those teams. I don't know what underlying motive I had. But whatever the motive was, it was for nothing. I didn't help either team in any positive way. I just took up a spot, that's all.

I could've done much better in school if I only would've had the motivation to learn. The actual learning portion of the school wasn't hard. It was my thinking and attitude that blocked me from learning what I should've learned. It was my "what's the use" attitude that kept me from doing better than I did.

Looking back now, if I'm honest with myself, I can't blame my not doing good in school on the teachers. They did what they were paid to do. They did their jobs correctly. They taught us what they were supposed to teach us.

I can't blame the bullies either for my not doing well in school. It was my fault for allowing them to do what they did.

I didn't learn this until years after high school. But someone told me, "Hurting people hurt people". So what those bullies were doing to me through all those years of school was getting all their hurt, pain, confusion, anger, regret, fear, and bitterness out of them and venting it onto me.

None of us knew that fact back then. Had I known that at the time, I may have been able to deal with that situation differently.

But as I was going through my school years, not knowing then what I know now, I just wanted them to stop. There was no abuse hotline. There was no bully support group where you could comfort each other or whatever they did. You just dealt with the situation however you chose to deal with it. And, like I said before, I dealt with my school bullies in the worst way that I could have.

So the question is, if I can't blame my not doing well in school on my teachers, and if I can't blame it on my bullies, then who can I blame it on? Whose fault is it? ME! It's my fault that I didn't do good in school!

I had the same opportunity to learn as every other student had. Those teachers were teaching the same material to every student in those classes.

The fact is, some students apply themselves. They actually want to learn what they're being taught. While other students don't apply themselves, they don't want to learn.

I was one of the students that didn't apply myself. I didn't care about what they were teaching. I have no one to blame but me. I threw away that good education by just going through the motions and by just doing as much as I had to just to get by.

I could've been anything I wanted to be had I applied myself in school, but I didn't. And because I didn't, I wasted too many years of my life just existing and not living.

For years after high school, I was just going through the day-to-day motions of life. I was doing nothing positive, nothing productive with my life. I was just taking up space in this world. I wasn't doing any good for anyone.

It's not that I wanted to just exist, to just take up space in this world. I couldn't help it. I was trapped in my own mental prison. The "I don't care. What's the use" attitude had me bound up.

You've heard the saying "Sticks and stones may break my bones, but names will never hurt me." I want you to know something. That saying is a lie. How do I know this? Because I've experienced it.

Think about it. When you get physically hurt, regardless of who you are, whether you're thick-skinned or thin-skinned, assertive or passive, secure about yourself or insecure about yourself, outgoing or an introvert, popular or a loner, that physical pain usually heals up within a couple of days or a couple of weeks.

On the other hand, when it comes to names, that's a different story. When you have someone who's thin-skinned, shy, a loner, or insecure about themselves, the wrong words hurt.

When other people laugh at you, ridicule you, and say hurtful words towards you, whether they mean what they say or are just joking around, it penetrates the heart and mind of a thin-skinned, insecure person. It goes down into the soul of the person. And depending on the person, it can take years to heal. And sadly, sometimes, the person never heals from it.

Names such as loser, stupid, and you'll never amount to anything they hurt. If you hear words like that long enough, often enough, you start believing it. You can start having all sorts of negative, destructive attitudes. You can start losing hope real quick.

And that's what happened to me. I was mentally beaten up, broken, and hopeless. I didn't see any bright, positive future for myself. I didn't have any positive hopes or dreams that I wanted to accomplish. I didn't know what I wanted to do as a job or career with my life.

As my life was steadily, unknowingly, going down the path of despair and destruction, something good actually happened in my life. I graduated high school.

In spite of everything that happened in school, by the grace of God and only by the grace of God, in June of 1982, I received my high school diploma from Richland High School in Gibsonia, Pennsylvania.

Sometime before graduation, they put up a list of all the students that were going to graduate that year. I was really hoping that my name was on that list. It was a relief to me that it was.

I don't know what I would've done if my name wasn't on that list. I couldn't deal with going through another year of school.

It was only God who helped me stay in school and do enough of the school work to graduate. Without God's help, I would've never made it.

So there I was, a high school graduate. Twelve years of school are behind me, and my whole life is ahead of me.

Although I had a piece of paper saying that I graduated high school, I was as unprepared as I could be to face the rest of my life.

I was leaving high school confused, fearful, and insecure about myself. I was leaving with no goals and no idea what I wanted to do with my life. I was leaving high school mentally broken, with an "I don't care. What's the use" attitude.

When I was supposed to be a responsible young man, I was mentally a scared little kid in a man's body. I mentally had no chance of succeeding. I was doomed to fail!

However, back then, at that time, I didn't realize the state that I was in when I left high school. So whether I was ready or not, my adult life was about to start. Let the disaster begin.

CHAPTER 2

Musical Jobs

WHILE I WAS IN SCHOOL, I got my first job. I was working as a dishwasher/busboy at a restaurant in Wexford, Pennsylvania, called Cimmaron. It was a good job. There was a lot of room for promotion.

However, I didn't last at Cimmaron very long. Why not? Because of my mental instability. My mind frame was keeping me bound up because of what was going on in school. My "what's the use" attitude was blocking me from caring about anything.

I didn't see any bright future for myself. And because I didn't see any good future for myself, I just went through the motions. I did just enough to get by. I was unmotivated. I had no reason to work hard.

You know how some people have goals, dreams, and ambitions for their lives. For example, they want to take over the family business, or they want to start a business of their own, or they want to make a million dollars by a certain age, or they want to retire by a certain age; I wasn't one of those people.

Also, the people who know exactly what career they want to have. They have a passion for being a doctor, a lawyer, a fireman, a police officer, a chef, an electrician, a painter, a social worker, or whatever it is. I wasn't one of those people either. I had absolutely no goals, dreams, or ambitions for my life.

Please don't get me wrong. Having goals, dreams, and ambitions is a wonderful thing. Whatever they are for you, keep them. Hold on to them. Don't let anyone talk you out of them.

Use whatever goals, dreams, and ambitions you have as motivation, as a reason to stay focused and to work hard.

Don't let anyone tell you that you can't do it or that it's stupid or whatever. If you want it bad enough and it means something to you, there's no one who can hinder you from achieving it but you.

So there I was, working at Cimmaron, unmotivated, just going through the motions. The problem was that I would carry this negative, destructive attitude into my adult life. And this negative, destructive attitude would become a job killer for me.

I took all that anger, frustration, confusion, fear, shame, embarrassment, regret, hopelessness, and scared little kid in a man's body-mind frame out of school with me into my adult life. And I let all that ruin some good jobs that could've turned into lifelong careers.

The first job I had after I graduated high school was going into the Air Force. I joined the Air Force in 1985 while I was living in Gibsonia, Pennsylvania.

Why I joined the Air Force is beyond me. It was the wrong choice for me.

Please don't think that I'm speaking badly about the Air Force or any other branch of the military. I'm certainly not doing that. As a matter of fact, the military, any branch of the military, is an honorable career. We need our military.

All I'm saying is, for me personally, joining the Air Force at that time in my life, with the mind frame that I had, wasn't going to work. It was a failure waiting to happen.

I was just coming out of high school with all that emotional baggage weighing me down. I was in my own mental prison.

Even though it was the wrong choice, even though I was in my own mental prison, there was no turning back now.

After going through the physical, passing all the tests, and being sworn in, I was off to basic training at Lackland Air Force Base in San Antonio, Texas.

My job when I was in the service was going to be a security specialist. Think about it; I, an insecure, passive, hopeless, mentally broken, scared little kid in a man's body, was going to be guarding the Air Force Bases and the planes. What a joke! Talk about choosing the wrong job at that time.

Looking back now, I'm glad it didn't work out back then. Why am I glad about that? Because I wasn't ready. I wasn't mentally ready for the responsibility of that job. I wasn't the right person to guard the bases and planes back then.

Had I been a responsible adult instead of a scared little kid in a man's body, had I been in my right mind instead of being in a mental prison, then the Air Force would've been a great career for me. However, it wasn't meant to be. It was the right job at the wrong time.

It didn't matter if I was a responsible adult or not or if I was in my right mind or not. It didn't change the fact that I was in the Air Force in basic training at Lackland Air Force Base.

For me personally, there was nothing physically hard about basic training. It was all about learning how to make a proper bed, how to march in unison, the proper way to salute, and learning the ins and outs of serving in the Air Force.

The trouble for me was all mental. It was my "I don't care. What's the use." attitude. It was my negative outlook on life. I saw no positive, productive future for myself.

In spite of my mental blockage, God helped me to get through basic training. So with basic training behind me, I was off to tech school. It was time for me to learn how to become a security specialist in the United States Air Force.

Again, for me personally, there was nothing physically hard about tech school. It was all about learning the proper way to read an ID badge, the proper way to deal with suspicious things on the bases, and the proper ways to deal with whatever we might encounter on the job.

The problem was me! My body was there, but my mind and my heart weren't. My past had me bound up. I was allowing my school years to have a stranglehold over my life. And it wasn't letting go.

I allowed my past to have a destructive power over my life that it had no business having! That decision ruined a lot of good things in my life, including my time in the Air Force and other jobs after that.

So there I was in tech school, learning how to be a security specialist. Toward the end of my time in school, I started to get a severe rash on my hands and my arms. The doctors called it either eczema or dermatitis. They told me that it would come and go for the rest of my life.

The rash that I had on me at that time was a bad one. So when I was twelve days away from graduating from tech school to become a security specialist, The Air Force discharged me. They gave me an entry-level discharge. My time in the Air Force was over. I was in there for four months.

It was a relief that they discharged me. I'm not mad that they let me go. They were doing me a favor. Why do I call it a favor? Because, like I said before, I wasn't ready. I wasn't a responsible adult. I wasn't mentally prepared for the responsibility of having the lives of people and the equipment that was on the bases in my hands.

Had I made it through Tech school, the Air Force was going to station me at Nellis Air Force Base in Las Vegas, Nevada.

That may or may not have been a good thing. Why do I say that? Because years later, when I was homeless in Reno, Nevada, during my psych years, I became addicted to gambling.

So had I been a security specialist in the Air Force stationed in Las Vegas addicted to gambling, that could've turned out really bad.

But that's not what God had planned for me. He saw that trouble on the horizon and removed me from that situation.

So the Air Force was behind me. Where do I go? What do I do now? What I do now is go to Sarasota, Florida, and live with my brother Jeff.

My mom was also living in Sarasota, Florida. She moved down to Sarasota after she got divorced from my stepdad, George. She moved there while I was still in high school, living in Gibsonia, Pennsylvania.

While my mom was living in Sarasota, she met a man named Roger. Roger was a Sarasota police officer at that time. Over the course of time, Roger and Mom fell in love. So in October of 1984, they got married. My brother Jeff and I went to their wedding. It was a nice ceremony.

There I was in Sarasota, Florida, just discharged from the Air Force, not knowing what I wanted to do with my life. I still had absolutely no goals for my life. I was clueless about what to do or where to go.

I was just discharged out of the best career that I ever could've had. Now, I had to start completely over in a city that I knew nothing about.

However, God didn't leave me completely alone. He already had my mom and my brother there before me. And that came in real handy for me. The Lord had my brother down in Sarasota so that I could live with him. He also had my mom down there to help me get a job.

The job Mom helped me get in Sarasota was at Phillippi Creek Oyster Bar. That's a seafood restaurant that serves really good food.

What can I say about Philippi Creek Oyster Bar? It was the funnest job that I ever had. I was just too bound up to realize it at the time.

Philippi Creek was a place where you could be yourself. You didn't have to be who the owners, managers, or coworkers wanted you to be. Most of the people that worked there were friendly. It was almost like one big family.

Just like the Air Force, Philippi Creek could've been the right job for me. But I got it at the wrong time in my life.

I was mentally unstable. I was undisciplined within myself. And I was definitely unfocused. I was lost spiritually. I was lost mentally. And I was lost emotionally. I was a mess just trying to fake it through.

The thing about it is, from the outside, you really couldn't tell how messed up I was on the inside. It was hard to tell what was going on with me on the inside. Why? Because burying my feelings by this point in my life was second nature to me. It was just the natural, instinctive thing for me to do when a negative situation came up in my life.

I was still that same ticking time bomb from my school years. And my fuse was getting shorter and shorter with every passing day.

Working at Phillippi Creek Oyster Bar could've been a good, fun, long-term job had it been under different circumstances. But it wasn't meant to be.

I was restless. I was looking for something better, something more fulfilling.

Have you ever heard the saying "The grass is always greener on the other side"? I'm here to tell you from experience that saying is not always true. As a matter of fact, more than half the time, you're better off exactly where you're at.

As I was working at Phillippi Creek, I was looking for greener pastures elsewhere. I quit and got rehired four times while I was working at Phillippi Creek.

During the times I wasn't working there, I had four other jobs while I was living in Sarasota. One job was working at a car wash. One job was working at K-Mart. And two of the jobs were working in other restaurants. One of the restaurants was called 1776. And the other was called Sarasota Brewing Company.

I remember when I was working at K-Mart. There was a coworker there whose name was Divita. I started to like her. She was at least six inches shorter than me. Why do I bring up her height? Because I mentally made it an issue.

Remember, I was very insecure about myself. I actually cared about what people said about me and what people thought about me. I made the mistake of taking it to heart.

I know that when two people are secure about themselves, about who they are, then a situation like this, one of the two more than six inches shorter or taller than the other, would not affect their relationship. What other people said or thought wouldn't affect them in any way.

On the other hand, when one of the two people in the relationship has an insecurity problem, that ruins the relationship.

Divita was secure about herself. Just like Jeannie when I was in junior high school. She was secure about herself. I was the problem in both situations. I was the weak link.

I don't know if either of those relationships would've gone anywhere. I don't know what Jeannie or Divita were feeling toward me. Regardless of how they were feeling toward me, I mentally put a stop to it. I ruined it, not them. It was my fault, not theirs.

I also remember one major situation that happened while I was working at the Sarasota Brewing Company.

The day this happened, it was an average day at work. There was nothing wrong or hard about this job. It was me, and my messed-up thinking that was the problem.

So on this particular day, I was in the kitchen doing my job. I was helping to cook and prepare the food for the customers. All of a sudden, we get a notice that the health inspectors are coming in to inspect the restaurant that day.

So we started to get the place ready for the inspection. We started cleaning up our areas. We started covering everything that needed to be covered. Everything that needed to be done, we were doing it.

All of a sudden, out of nowhere, a thought came into my messed-up head. The thought was, "Why are we cleaning up our areas and covering everything that needs to be covered just to pass the health inspection? Why aren't we doing these things as an everyday part of our job?"

Well, with me being depressed, bound up, hopeless, and seeing no bright, positive future for myself anyway, I quit.

Did I mess up? Yes! Did I leave them in a bind? Yes! But at that time in my life, I didn't care. I wasn't thinking straight. I wasn't in my right mind. I was in a pit of confusion, despair, and doubt.

So that day at Sarasota Brewing Company, I didn't discuss it with anybody, and I didn't get anybody's advice. I just walked out the front door.

I didn't think about the pros and cons of that decision. I didn't think about any future repercussions of that decision. I just made a spur-of-the-moment choice, and I went with it.

I made a lot of bad decisions in my life. Some were big, and some were small. But too many of my bad decisions affected other people in a harmful way.

My time at Sarasota Brewing Company came to a crashing halt. That seems like the theme of my life: things coming to a crashing halt.

While I was living in Sarasota, still working at Philippi Creek, I did something I was sure was going to work. I went into a phone booth and looked through the business advertisement section of the Yellow Pages, one page at a time.

What would cause me to do such a thing? What was I looking for? I was looking for a spark. I was looking, page by page, for a job, for a career that might spark my interest.

At that time in my life, I had no goals, I had no ambitions, and I had no focus in my life. I was just existing, not living. I was just going through the day-to-day motions.

I saw no light in my future. So if I could find a spark of interest in one of the jobs in this Yellow Pages phone book, I might find a sliver of light. I had nothing to lose. So why not try?

You might think if someone did something like this, they would find something. They would find at least one job that would pique their interest. That would be a fair statement, am I right? Of the hundreds of business advertisements that were in the Yellow Pages, at least one of them would spark an interest. At least one of them would seem interesting enough to at least try.

But you know what I found? NOTHING! No spark, no flicker, no fire, no interest in any of the jobs that were in that book.

I went into that phone booth, grasping at straws. I left that phone booth empty-handed. I was no better off coming out of that phone booth than I was going into it.

I came out of that phone booth with one conclusion. Every job has its good points and bad points. Whether you're a doctor, a lawyer, a cook, an electrician, a garbageman, or whatever, there are positives and negatives to that job. It's all about your mind frame.

I was back to square one. I had no hope. I had no idea what I wanted to do or where I wanted to go.

I was in a very dangerous position at this point. I was in a mental prison. My past still had a stranglehold over my life. I was in a pit of despair and hopelessness. I was a walking time bomb whose fuse was getting shorter and shorter.

Life to me was useless; it was meaningless. My life had no value to me. It was worthless. I didn't care if I lived or died. As a matter of fact, death would've been a good thing. Death at that point in my life would've been like a friend. It would've been doing me a favor in taking me.

Please don't get me wrong. My life was not a twenty-four-hour-a-day, seven-day-a-week pit of darkness and death. There were times of laughter and good times. I even had a good idea that could've helped a lot of people.

This idea came to me while I was in Sarasota working at Phillippi Creek. My idea was not a "normal" idea. Then again, I wasn't a "normal" thinking person either.

My idea was to run around the country for the American Heart Association. I didn't say across the country, but around it—from Florida to Maine, from Maine to Washington State, from Washington State to California, and from California to Florida.

I don't remember where this idea came from. I don't remember if it was something I read or something I heard or something I saw. But the idea was in my head. And to me, it seemed like a good idea.

Why I chose the American Heart Association because of the heart surgeries I went through as a child. It was a good, reputable organization. And going through the heart surgeries, it just seemed like the right thing to do.

As good as this idea was, I had one major problem standing in the way of this run being accomplished.

That problem was my messed-up mind! Not only was I confused, insecure about myself, and bound up, but I was also lazy!

I wanted this idea, running around the country for the American Heart Association, to happen. But

I didn't want to put the physical effort into getting it done.

I would've had to train like I never trained for a run before. I would've had to discipline myself and give this a 100 percent wholehearted effort. The motivation was there. The desire was there. But nothing else was.

The problem was I wasn't taking this run seriously like I should've been. I needed to give this a wholehearted effort. However, I wasn't even giving this a half-hearted effort. My mind, my heart, and my body were not on the same page like they needed to be.

It was a legitimate idea that could've helped a lot of people. I was too physically lazy to make it happen. That was just one more thing that came to a crashing halt.

As I was an employee at Phillippi Creek, I heard other people talking about getting married, having kids, and buying their own house.

They were talking about good, positive things. They were talking about what most responsible adults think about. They were talking about the American dream.

However, at that time in my life, I wasn't even thinking about getting married, having kids, or owning my own house.

It was good for them to do because they were in their right mind. I wasn't! I was angry, depressed, confused, hopeless, and a scared little kid in a man's body.

I was not husband material. I didn't care about anyone, including myself. How can I love a wife if I don't even care about her? I can't!

As far as having kids go, how can I have kids of my own when I was mentally and emotionally a kid myself? Again, I can't!

Also, owning my own house, that definitely wasn't going to happen back then. I was just existing, just going through the day-to-day motions.

I didn't know where I wanted to go or what I wanted to do with my life. So putting down roots and buying my own house would've been useless for me to do.

Back then, the American dream wasn't meant to happen for me. I wasn't mentally and emotionally ready for the responsibility of taking care of and providing for a wife and kids.

I also wasn't responsible enough to make monthly payments on a house of my own.

As you can tell, my having any sort of a deep, personal, intimate relationship with anyone wasn't happening. If I would've tried, it would've been hurtful to them in the end.

So when it came to the area of sex, I went to prostitutes and strippers to handle that need.

There was one main reason why I went to prostitutes and strippers to fulfill my sexual needs. That one main reason was this: it was strictly business, nothing else.

There was nothing personal about it. When the business was over, we went our separate ways. There was no jealousy. There was no sneaking around each other's backs. When it was over, she went one way, and I went the other.

Some people might be asking, "Wasn't I afraid of getting robbed or catching a disease or getting killed?" No, I wasn't.

With the messed-up mind I had, I wasn't even thinking about getting robbed or catching a disease. And as far as getting killed, I was ready to die anyway. They would've been doing me a favor. They would've kept me from going through a lot of mental and emotional hurt and pain.

Was I right in going to prostitutes and strippers to meet my sexual needs? It depends on who you ask.

But as far as I was concerned, I was a worldly person with no bright future. So I was alright with it.

Would I do the same thing now? No. I wouldn't do it now for one reason. I'm a Christian. The Bible is against sex outside marriage.

Like I said before, working at Phillippi Creek Oyster Bar was the funnest place I've ever worked at. As long as you were doing your job, the owners didn't mess with you. As a matter of fact, the owners took care of the employees who worked there.

I remember one time while I was working there, the owners of the restaurant actually closed the place down for one day. They closed the restaurant that day to take all the employees who were working there at that time on a one-day Sea Escape cruise.

What happened was this. Everybody met at the restaurant early that morning. We all got on either two or three buses that the owners had waiting for us. The buses were then driven to the place where the cruise was departing from. (Where the cruise departed from, I can't remember.)

All I remember about the cruise was I did some drinking, I did some gambling, and I had a nice meal. It was a fun day, a good cruise.

Once the cruise was over, we all got back on the buses and headed back to Phillippi Creek.

As I was working at Phillippi Creek, there was one thing that happened to me on my birthday that caught me totally off guard.

Who came up with this idea, how they came up with this idea, how long they were planning this idea, I'll never know. I don't know how they kept it a secret like they did.

What happened was this. As I was working in the kitchen, helping to cook the food for the customers, two of the waitresses came in escorted me to the restaurant area and set me on a barstool.

Out of nowhere, right in the middle of the restaurant, right in front of the customers and all, in walks a stripper. Was she truly a stripper? I don't know. I never saw her before.

Regardless of whether she was or wasn't, she stood right in front of me (and everybody else in the restaurant at the time) and did a strip dance for me. Obviously, she didn't take a lot off because it was a public restaurant with kids in there eating.

I do remember she wore a garter on her leg. And she wanted me to get the garter off her leg with my teeth.

I was having trouble getting it off, so she helped me a little bit. Eventually, with her help, I finally got it off her leg.

That was the most off-the-wall birthday surprise that I ever had in my life—absolutely caught me off guard. I never saw it coming.

But that's what I'm saying. Most of the good things, the good times that happened to me at a job, was at Phillippi Creek Oyster Bar. I was just too bound up, too blinded to see it.

Despite the good things that happened to me at Phillippi Creek, there was one major negative question that came into my head while I was working there also. And this one question was about to turn my life upside down.

CHAPTER 3

Psych

Have you ever asked yourself the question, "Why am I here? What's my purpose on this earth?"

I asked myself that question at a time in my life when I was lost and when I was without any direction when I saw no bright future for my life.

Up to that point, my life was an emotional and mental roller coaster. Most of my days were mentally and emotionally tough, with me being in a state of fear, confusion, and an "I don't care. What's the use" attitude.

However, there were also a few days every once in a while when my life actually seemed good—when my life actually seemed bearable.

All of a sudden, that question came into my mind and plunged my life into a pit of despair, death, and revenge.

ONE LAST STRING TO CUT

That question tried to finish off what those school bullies started. If it wasn't for Jesus being my last string, that question would've finished me off.

I was working at Phillippi Creek Oyster Bar in Sarasota, Florida, when that question came to me. It was either 1989 or 1990 as I was in the kitchen helping to cook the food for the customers when, out of nowhere, that question popped into my head: "Why am I here? What's my purpose on this earth?"

I was in a very fragile state of mind. And it wasn't going to take a lot to push me over the edge. And like I said, without Jesus being my last string, this question was going to be the death of me (and other people as well).

I thought about that question for a week or two. But I couldn't come up with a good answer. I couldn't come up with a good reason why I was here on this earth. I had no idea why I was here. I had no idea what my purpose was.

I had no idea what I wanted to do with my life or where I wanted to go. Since I saw my life going nowhere, since I saw no positive future for my life, and since I was just taking up space and not helping society in any positive, productive way, I just thought I would end the mental and emotional pain, fear, and confusion that I was in. I'd kill myself. I'd end this day-to-day existence that I was going through.

I was living with my brother Jeff in Sarasota, Florida, when this idea came into my head.

The first way I was going to kill myself was with a knife. I had a knife in my room. I put the knife right under my rib cage. All I had to do was push the knife up, and my life would've been over.

But God had other ideas. He kept me from killing myself. He had plans for my life that I knew nothing about. I was trying to end my life while he wanted to save it. The thing about it was I had no idea God was working behind the scenes to save my life.

So there I was stuck. I couldn't kill myself. Now what do I do? I wanted to die, but now how do I do it?

Here comes the next idea in my messed-up mind. If I couldn't kill myself, I'd make the state do it for me. I'll kill someone else so that the state will kill me.

Was that a rational thought? Absolutely not! I'm not denying or disputing that.

However, I wasn't in a rational state of mind. I didn't care about anything or anyone, including myself. I had a "what's the use" attitude. I saw nothing good happening in my future. I was in the mind frame of "I have nothing to lose."

If someone had to die by my hands for me to die, so be it. That's just how it had to be.

As I said, I was living with my brother Jeff when this thought came into my head. So just as a matter of convenience, he was going to be my ticket to death row.

I remember the night that I was going to do this. I not only had a knife in my room, but I also had a gun as well. I had to wait till he went to bed. After midnight, when I thought enough time had passed for him to fall asleep, I went into my room and got my gun. But I couldn't go through with it. God wouldn't let me do it (which was a good thing).

Now what do I do? I couldn't kill myself. I couldn't kill my brother. I still wanted to die. I was stuck again.

So the next illogical idea that came into my messed up mind was to find my school bullies and kill them.

I blamed them for my life being so messed up anyway. In my mind, they caused all the mental pain that I was feeling. So they should pay for it.

I could get my revenge on them. I could find them and torture them to death. I could kill them slowly, causing as much physical pain to them as possible. I could look into their eyes and see the terror that they were going through.

But there was one problem with this plan. I didn't put any time or effort into finding any of them. I couldn't torture and kill them if I didn't know where they were.

I was back to square one. I still wanted to die. However, I couldn't kill myself, I couldn't kill my brother, I couldn't kill my school bullies. Now what do I do?

If the state was going to kill me, someone had to die by my hands. So my last irrational, illogical plan was to kill anybody. Any random person on the street was going to be my ticket to death row.

This is where the psych hospital phase of my life starts. When the idea of wanting to die came into my head, psych hospitals became a part of my life.

The first psych hospital that I went into was either in 1990 or 1991 while I was living with my sister in Michigan.

During this first time in the hospital, I was only in there for one weekend. On Monday morning, they took me in to see the doctor. Here I am, being new to the psych system. I have no idea what the system can do for me, no idea how they can help me. It was a brand-new experience for me. I had no idea what to expect.

So there I am, talking to the doctor, telling him about my problem. I'll never forget what he told me. He told me out of his own mouth that I should stop and smell the roses.

I'll tell you something: that's not what I was expecting to hear. Yes, this was a new experience for me. Yes, I had no idea what they could do for me or how or if they could help me. But for him to tell me to stop and smell the roses wasn't what I was expecting. I wanted to die, not smell any roses.

Sometime that same day, I was discharged from that psych hospital. As you can imagine, I was no better off leaving the hospital than I was going into it. I was still on the same path of death and destruction.

So what do I do now? I was still a ticking time bomb whose fuse was getting shorter and shorter by the day. I had no idea what I wanted to do with my life or where I wanted to go. I was hopeless, and I wanted to die. I was in a world of hurt. I was in a very dangerous time in my life.

So what did I decide to do when they discharged me out of the hospital? I'm off to Reno, Nevada. What would prompt me to go to Reno? The Mustang Ranch. What exactly is the Mustang Ranch? It's a legal prostitution house.

My plan was to go to Reno, Nevada, and visit the Mustang Ranch. After my visit to the ranch, I was planning somehow to end my life.

However, I had a major problem with this plan. The problem wasn't getting to Reno because I did get there. The problem was going to the Mustang Ranch. I didn't have the money to go there. When I arrived in Reno, I had 7$ in my pocket. And that definitely wasn't enough money to visit the ranch.

As you can tell, my Reno/Mustang Ranch trip wasn't logically planned out. It was definitely spur of the moment. And it failed miserably. It was doomed to fail from the start; I just didn't realize it.

Let me ask you a question. Have you ever had a plan that you didn't plan out logically, but it was just a spur-of-the-moment plan? How did it work out for you? Did it fail miserably like mine did or did it somehow succeed?

There, I was stuck in Reno, Nevada. I didn't know anybody there. And I didn't know my way around the city. So I walked into a bar and ordered a beer. After I finished my beer, I walked to the nearest payphone, called 911, and went into the next psych hospital I went to.

I don't remember how long I was in that particular hospital. But it wasn't more than three days, and they discharged me.

I was alone in a strange city, wanting to die. That was a recipe for disaster. If it wasn't for God unknowingly working behind the scenes in my life, it could've turned out a lot differently. It could've ended with people dying, including me. But again, God was over that situation, protecting everyone.

So there I was in Reno, Nevada, with no money and nowhere to stay. This was my first time being homeless.

In Reno, there are three places for homeless people to stay for the night. The first place is the Salvation Army. The second place is the Reno/Sparks Gospel Mission. And the third place is some church that I don't remember the name of.

I've stayed in all three places when I could get in them. When I couldn't get in any of these places, I slept behind buildings, in between buildings, and under balconies. For a homeless person, almost anywhere is a potential place to sleep.

A good thing about Reno is that the casinos are open twenty-four hours a day, seven days a week. Why do I bring this up? Because for a homeless person who can't get into one of the shelters, a casino is another place for shelter. You can spend the night watching television. And if you get too tired, you can go into one of the bathroom stalls and get a quick power nap.

The thing about the Salvation Army and the Reno/Sparks Gospel Mission is that you can only stay there at nighttime. During the day, you have to leave. You can't be there until they open back up that night.

So during the day, the homeless people had to find some place to go. They had to find something to do till the shelters opened back up.

There were different things to do in Reno. For example, you could go into the casinos and watch sports on television. Or you could go to a casino called Circus Circus and watch the circus acts. Or you could walk around town collecting aluminum cans for a little extra money. Or you could go to the public library and hang out for the day.

Personally, my favorite way to pass the day was at the library. I had a very specific reason to be at the library. It was to collect the names of my role models. Who were my role models back then? Serial killers and mass murderers.

I was spending hours at the library collecting names of serial killers and mass murderers from all over the world who killed anywhere from three people and up.

I was putting their names in a little notebook that I carried around with me everywhere I went.

At one time, I had over four hundred names in my notebook.

Was this a normal thing to collect? Absolutely not! Normal people collect things such as stamps or coins. But I wasn't normal.

I was obsessed with death. I wanted to die, but God wouldn't let me. He still had a plan and a purpose for my life that I knew nothing about.

I wanted to be a serial killer or a mass murderer. I wanted to be a Timothy McVeigh, a Ted Bundy, a Green River Killer.

I had anger, hatred, confusion, fear, and hopelessness inside me, controlling me. I was living in a prison of pain and regret—a prison of a wasted, unfruitful life. Life meant nothing to me, mine or anyone else's.

There I was in Reno, doing what I've always done, just going through the day-to-day motions. I was just taking up space in this world, not living at all but just existing.

Even though I was obsessed with death, even though I wanted to be a serial killer or a mass murderer, no one would've ever realized it from the outside. I was able to function "normally" around other people.

Remember, it was second nature for me to bury my feelings. I didn't carry my feelings on my sleeves.

I didn't show my negative feelings very often. I pretty much kept them to myself.

While I was in Reno, I actually got a job. It would turn out to be my last job before I went to prison.

I got a job at a Casino called Club Cal Neva as a dishwasher. I only worked there for maybe one or two months. It was sometime in early 1994.

Almost every night after I got done working, I would go to the poker machines and start gambling and drinking.

So in the beginning of 1994, with me hating my job anyway, plus the fact that I wasn't saving any money, I quit my dishwashing job at Club Cal Neva.

I bought a bus ticket at the Greyhound bus station and headed back to Florida.

I have to say that while I was in Reno, God was working on my heart. How was he doing that? Through the Reno/Sparks Gospel Mission. That's one of the homeless shelters in Reno.

To eat supper and/or sleep there for the night, you had to sit through a gospel message. The mission had someone come in every night to speak the Word of God to everyone who was going to eat and/or sleep there that night.

Jesus was knocking on my heart through those nightly messages. He wanted to come into my heart to be my Savior and Lord.

However, it would be another ten years before I let him into my heart. It was another ten wasted, unfruitful years before Jesus got my full, undivided attention while I was in prison.

So what would cause me to not accept him as my Savior and Lord while I was at the Reno/Sparks Gospel Mission? Two words: peer pressure!

The people that I was hanging around with back then were unsaved. So had I accepted Jesus back then, they might have kicked me to the curb.

I was in a very delicate state of mind. I didn't need anyone or anything pushing me over the edge. If the people I was hanging around with would've turned their back on me, there's no telling what I would've done.

So I allowed my wanting to be accepted by them to stop me from receiving Jesus.

I realize that had I received Jesus into my heart back then in Reno, he would've taken care of me. However, it was the peer pressure of me wanting to be accepted by my friends that kept me from Jesus. Yes, I made the wrong choice. I chose my friends over Jesus.

Let me say something about peer pressure, about wanting to be accepted by your friends. That is a very dangerous situation to be in. It's dangerous because they may be the "wrong" crowd to be around. They may have you doing things that you don't want to do—or doing things that you have no business doing.

Think about this: If you do something that you have no business doing just because they're pressuring you into doing it. And you get caught, not them, just you. Do you actually think that any of them are going to be there for you? Do you actually think that any of them are going to help you get out of the trouble you're in? I highly doubt it. More than likely, you're on your own.

I've learned from experience that peer pressure, that wanting to be accepted by your friends, keeps you from being who you're meant to be. It keeps you from being the real you, the person that God created you to be.

Don't let other people tell you who you are or tell you who they want you to be. Be you! Be the unique, one-of-a-kind person that God created you to be.

If anyone laughs at you or talks bad about you because you didn't bow down to peer pressure, don't worry about it. Don't lose any sleep over it. If they're laughing at you or talking bad about you, they're showing their own insecurities about themselves.

So I left Reno, Nevada, in early 1994. That started me on a trip—a trip of traveling around the country on a Greyhound bus, seeing different psych hospitals from the inside.

I was obsessed with death. I was homicidal and suicidal with an "I don't care. What's the use" attitude.

From 1994 until 2001, I took a Greyhound bus from the death penalty state to the death penalty state that had a lethal injection.

My plan was simple. Go to a state that had the death penalty by lethal injection, kill at least one person, and have the state put me out of my misery.

It was a simple plan with one big problem. Every time I got to the state I wanted to go to, I couldn't go through with it. The thought was there. The motivation was there. The intention was there. But I couldn't do it. I couldn't physically kill anybody.

So what would I end up doing? Going to the nearest pay phone and calling 911. They'd send the police to get me and take me to the next psych hospital.

My plan was to die and take people with me. However, God's plan wasn't the same as my plan. He had his own plan that was totally opposite of mine. I wanted to die, but he wanted me to live. He wanted me to live not only physically but also spiritually. He was working behind the scenes, keeping me from physically hurting anyone, including myself.

I've been in at least fourteen different psych hospitals in seven different states: one in Pennsylvania, one in Michigan, one in North Carolina, one in Oklahoma, one in Arkansas, one in Nevada, and eight in Florida.

I have at least four different diagnoses, which are schizoaffective disorder, schizophrenia, bipolar disorder, and major depression.

I've been on a lot of different medications—a few of these are Thorazine, Haldol, and lithium.

But you know what, with all the hospitals that I've been in, all the doctors that I saw, all the medications that I took, I've never gotten any better. I was just as suicidal, just as homicidal, just as confused and obsessed with death, leaving all those hospitals as I was going into them.

There's a very good, eye-opening reason why I wasn't getting any better. I was misdiagnosed.

It wasn't the doctor's fault or the nurse's fault or anybody's fault. They were diagnosing me as having some sort of mental illness. And from the outside, that's exactly what it looked like. They were trying to treat something that I never had with medications that were never going to work.

What am I talking about? If being homicidal, suicidal, and obsessed with death isn't a mental illness, what else can it be? Evil spirits! I wasn't mentally ill. I was controlled by evil spirits.

All those doctors in all those hospitals were trying to heal me of an illness that they thought I had with medications and therapy that were never going to work. They were trying to heal something that was spiritual by physical means.

It wasn't their fault. They didn't know what it was. My family didn't know. I didn't know.

So how am I so sure that it was evil spirits and not mental illness? Because on September 30, 2003, at Tomoka Correctional Institution, when I truly received Jesus Christ as my Savior and Lord, the homicidal and suicidal thoughts and my obsession with death, they were gone. Jesus healed and delivered me from them. He did what the hospitals, Doctors, and medications couldn't do!

Now let me ask a question. How many people who seem to be mentally ill, that from the outside look to be mentally ill, are being misdiagnosed as well? How many of them are suffering from the same thing I did: evil spirits? I know I'm not the only one!

Some people might be saying, "I don't believe in evil spirits." What I would say to them is, "That's okay. You don't have to believe in them. However, just because you don't believe in them, it doesn't mean they're not real. I'm living proof that they are real, that they do exist."

As I was in my "mental illness" stage of life, going from state to state, from hospital to hospital, my family was still behind me. Why they were still behind me, still in my corner, helping me, supporting me, encouraging me, only God knows.

I don't deserve my family. All the grief, all the shame, all the embarrassment that I caused them. A lot of families have turned their back on other family members who have done a lot less than I did to mine.

I couldn't have blamed my family or been mad at my family if they would've kicked me to the curb. I would've deserved it. I would've had it coming to me. It's only by God's grace, his mercy, that they didn't.

There were multiple times when my family allowed me to stay with them during this period of my life. However, it never lasted very long. It wasn't their fault that it didn't last very long. It wasn't anything they did or said.

It didn't last very long because of me. I was too mentally unstable at that time. I was too restless. I was too driven by death, driven by revenge, to settle down.

It didn't only happen with my family. It also happened with a psych hospital in Florida that I was in as well. When they found places for me to live outside the hospital, I was just as mentally unstable, just as restless with their places as I was with my family.

I never stayed anywhere outside a hospital at that time in my life for more than a couple of weeks.

For example, when I was in Michigan, my sister found a place for us to stay. It lasted maybe two weeks, and I was gone.

When I was in Florida, my brother allowed me to stay with him. Again, within two or three weeks, I left.

My mom found me a place to live in Tampa, Florida. She took me shopping for a TV and some other things for the place. Within three or four days, I was gone.

One of the psych hospitals in Fort Myers, Florida, found me three different places to live. I left two of those places in less than a week. The third place, I may have made it two or three weeks. After that, I left.

I even tried staying with John, my friend from high school. He was living in Maryland at the time. He was staying with three or four other guys. They were all Christians sharing a place together. John allowed me to come up there from Florida to stay with him.

There was nothing wrong with the place or any of the guys that were living there. They were all nice, courteous, and friendly to me.

It was all me! My mind wasn't right. Within two weeks, I left. I was on a Greyhound bus back to Florida.

I want to point out something from my experience that a lot of people don't realize.

Did you notice that I was in different places with different people? And three times, I was by myself. And every time, whether I was with someone or by myself, I never lasted more than two or three weeks before I left.

What was the common thread in all those different situations? ME! In all those different situations, I was there.

So what am I saying? What am I trying to point out? Everywhere we go, we take us with us.

The good or the bad us. The positive or the negative us. The friendly or the hateful us. The lying us, the caring us, the drug addict us, the alcoholic us, the vengeful us.

Everywhere we go, we're taking our faults, flaws, and issues. We're taking our strengths and weaknesses.

We can run from people. We can run from situations. We can run from a lot of different things. However, we can never, ever run from ourselves!

If your life isn't going the way you want it to, if you're going from place to place, from job to job, from hospital to hospital, from rehab to rehab, from escape to escape, do you realize that you're taking you with you?

I've learned one very important lesson about this topic. You can go from place to place, rehab to rehab, hospital to hospital, escape to escape as long as you want to, hoping that your situation will eventually change, hoping that someone or something will make it all better for you.

The problem isn't your surroundings. It's not the people you're hanging around. The problem is you!

Until you change you, your situation isn't going to change. And how do you change yourself? It starts with a choice. You have to want to change.

You can go to every AA and NA meeting that they have. You can listen to motivational speakers.

You can go to self-help conferences. You can do a dozen other things.

But none of them is going to help you. None of them is going to help you until you choose to want help.

You have to get to a point in your own mind where you say, "Enough! I don't like the way my life is going, and it needs to change."

No one can make that choice for you. It's something that only you can make.

Have you ever heard the saying "When you hit rock bottom, the only way is up"? I want to tell you. That's a lie.

When you hit bottom, you just stay there until you choose not to. You stay on the bottom as long as you want to stay on the bottom, whether it's a day, a month, a year, or for the rest of your life. It's your choice, no one else's.

If you like being miserable, hateful, fearful, depressed, and in bondage to things that will never help you, then stay on the bottom right where you're at. But if you don't like being on the bottom, then do something about it.

Until we change our own mind frame, our own way of thinking about ourselves, our situation, our outlook on whatever needs to be changed, we're going to continue to be in bondage to our own mind, to our own thinking, to our own selves.

We have to realize that it starts with a choice. You have to want to change. If you don't want to, then it's never going to happen.

If you're tired of being on the bottom, if you're tired of the way your life is going, and you're making a choice to change, that could mean that God is knocking on your heart. That could mean that Jesus wants to come into your life.

I know from experience that Jesus is ready, willing, and able to help you. I know from experience that he's ready, willing, and able to be anything and everything that you need him to be.

He's the only one that was able to help me when I was at rock bottom. As miserable as I was, as nasty as I was, as depressed as I was, as lost as I was, he was the only one that was able to get me out of that dark, lonely pit of death and despair I was in.

Jesus saved, healed, and delivered me out of my negative situation. There's no doubt that he can do the same for you too.

Sometime during the mid-1990s, I took a Greyhound bus trip to Houston, Texas. I had a very specific reason for this trip. I was planning to do what I would eventually do five or six years later.

I had every intention of going to Houston, Texas, and carrying out my bank plan. My bank plan was simple. It was going into a bank with a machete and a hand grenade and getting an FBI agent sent to me. Once I had the FBI agent inside with me, I would kill them with the machete and get the Federal death penalty.

There I was, pulling into Houston on the Greyhound bus. As the bus was coming into the city, I saw the bank that I was going to do this at. It was right down the street from the bus station.

I got off the bus and walked directly to the bank. When I got to the bank, the war started in my mind. I stood outside the bank for a few minutes debating with myself. Do I or do I not go through with this plan? The yes, go through with the plan, won out.

So I walked into the bank and got cold feet. There was a security guard in the bank. I walked up to him and told him that I had a machete and a hand grenade in my duffel bags.

He did what he was supposed to do. He handcuffed me and called the police. The police came and took me to the Harris County Jail.

What can I say about the Harris County Jail? In my opinion, there are only two words that can describe that jail. And those two words are controlled chaos.

When they booked me into jail, there were hundreds of other people in there with me, waiting to be booked in as well.

There were people everywhere. Some people were on the floor; others were on the benches. Some were sleeping; others were awake. There were people coming and going. You had to step over the people that were sleeping on the floor.

Eventually, it was my turn to be booked into jail. Who I talked to, how long it took, what they asked and said, I don't know. The whole process was a blur.

After they processed me, they moved me up to where I was going to stay until my court date. They put me in with forty or fifty other guys. We were all in one big room.

Here I was, totally new to the system. I didn't know how the system worked or what to expect.

I was homicidal, suicidal, obsessed with death, skinny, shy, and alone. I didn't know anybody in there. And I didn't want to know anybody in there.

On the surface, that would seem like a recipe for disaster, a recipe for a lot of trouble. Being skinny, shy, alone, brand-new to the system, with a death wish in a Texas jail. The odds would be against that person to get out of that jail unscathed. To get out of that jail with nothing bad happening to them.

But God! If God wasn't with me in that jail, if he wouldn't have had his protection over me, I would've never made it out unscathed. He kept all those guys from doing any harm to me. It was nothing I did. It was everything he did that kept me safe in there.

They had religious services in the jail. Every time they called for religious services, I went. I was unsaved at the time. I wasn't looking for God at that time in my life. I went to the religious services just to get out of the room for a little while.

I wasn't looking for God or interested in God at that time in my life. But he was looking for and interested in me.

It would take another five-plus years before God would get my full, undivided attention. He just had to sit me down for almost twenty years to do it.

I was hardheaded, stubborn, and blinded. I didn't see what God was doing in my life. I wasn't listening to his promptings. I gave him no choice. I gave him no other option but to hit me over the head with his spiritual sledgehammer because I was stuck on stupid!

So there I was in the Harris County Jail. At this point, I've been in there for around two months. And they call me to court. I was about to see the judge. I had no idea what I was facing. I had no idea how serious the charges might be. I had no idea how much time I could get or was going to get.

But God! God was working behind the scenes. He was my defense attorney, and I didn't even know it. When it was my turn to stand in front of the Judge, he gave me time served. I was free to go.

So later that day, they processed me out of the Harris County Jail. Again, the only two words that I can use to describe the process would be organized chaos. There were hundreds of people being processed out at the same time in an organized manner that looked chaotic.

Every officer in there who was processing people into jail and processing people out of jail knew exactly what they were doing. They were like a well-oiled machine, knowing exactly what their job was and how to do it.

Harris County Jail is behind me now. Did I learn my lesson? No! Am I still stuck on stupid? Yes! I was no better coming out of that jail than I was going into it.

My psych years kept rolling on. The cycle kept going. A Greyhound bus trip to a death penalty state. Into another hospital. Out of another hospital. It was a vicious cycle that I had no power over. It had me as a prisoner, and it wasn't letting go. I was just along for the ride.

In the process of time, somewhere around 1999 or 2000, I decided to take one last trip to Reno, Nevada.

I was living in Fort Myers, Florida, when I came up with this spur-of-the-moment plan. I don't know where this plan came from.

All I know is the idea of going to Reno came into my head. It seemed like a good idea to me. I wasn't doing anything positive or productive at the time. I wasn't helping society in any good way. I was just existing, going through the day-to-day motions. In my illogical, messed-up thinking, a trip back to Reno, Nevada, wasn't the worst idea I could've come up with.

So I packed a few bags with some clothes, hygiene items, and a few personal things. Next, I went to the bank and withdrew all the money I had. Then I went to the Greyhound Bus station and bought my ticket to Reno.

It took around three days to get to Reno. But eventually, I got there. Once I got there, I put my bags in one of the bus terminal lockers. Then I got something to eat.

After I got something to eat, it was time to gamble.

I arrived in Reno with either $800 or $900 in my pocket.

ONE LAST STRING TO CUT

Why I was there and what I was trying to accomplish during this particular trip, I have no idea.

However, it didn't matter. I was there. For the next two and a half straight days, I went from one casino to another, playing one poker machine after another.

Two and a half days after I started, the $800 or $900 that I started with was now down to $12. It was just enough money to get my bags from the bus terminal locker.

There I was, a second time in Reno, Nevada, broke, homicidal, suicidal, depressed with a "what's the use" destructive attitude.

So I walked to the nearest pay phone and called 911. I was only in the psych hospital at that time for a couple of days.

They let me call my mom. She wired me enough money for a bus ticket back to Florida.

That would turn out to be my last bus trip as a "free man" for the next twenty-plus years. Why? Because, in less than two years, my time existing in society as a "free man" was about to come to a crashing halt.

My life was about to be drastically changed. I was about to go from the frying pan into the fire.

CHAPTER 4

Off to the School of Prison

BOOM! MAY 9, 2001—THAT'S THE day that the time bomb inside me exploded.

That's the day that all that anger, hatred, bitterness, fear, confusion, hopelessness, and all those other negative feelings and emotions that's been building up inside me since kindergarten came out of me and onto six innocent people who had nothing to do with anything that happened to me.

May 9, 2001, started like any other day for me. I woke up feeling confused, hopeless, and thinking about death.

So I packed two duffel bags with some of my personal property and headed for the city bus stop.

On the way into town, there's an Army/Navy store. The bus route passed right by it. I stopped at the store before going into town. I already had a machete in one of my bags. I stopped into the Army/Navy store to get a hand grenade. After getting the hand grenade, I proceeded the rest of the way into town.

The city bus stopped right in front of the bank. I got off the bus and headed for the bank.

Again, the debate started in my mind. "Am I or am I not going to do this?"

The desire was there. The motivation was there. The problem was, on the outside, physically, I'm a passive person. I don't like to engage in physical violence. On the other hand, mentally, I've killed people all day long. In my head, I've tortured a lot of people to death.

I wasn't used to doing anything like this. I was going into uncharted territory. I wasn't a career criminal. So this was a real war in my head.

There, I was headed for the front door of the bank. And the "don't do it" got a momentary win. So I got back on the city bus and rode it for a while.

Eventually, I'm back at the bank. There was a McDonald's right next to the bank. So I went to get something to eat. After I ate, I headed for the bank again.

It was a real mental battle. "Was I going into the bank and carrying out my plan, or wasn't I?"

After a major mental battle, I eventually ended up in the bank. I put my bags on the chairs in the lobby. A bank employee came and asked if I needed any help.

I pulled out the hand grenade and machete from my bag and told her to lock the front door. As we were headed for the front door, other people in the bank were leaving out the back door.

I guess as I was going into the bank, the security guard was out back doing whatever it was he was doing. It didn't take long for him to come in and ask me what was going on what I wanted.

My wants were easy. I only wanted two things—two people to be exact. The first person I wanted was a local news anchor. Her name was Lois Thome. I wanted her there so I could tell her my story.

The second person I wanted was an FBI agent. I wanted the FBI agent there so I could kill them and get the Federal death penalty.

The police started showing up real quick, taking up their positions, blocking off the street.

Eventually, the hostage negotiator got there. We started talking. He asked me what I wanted. I told him I wanted Lois Thome and an FBI agent.

After I told him what I wanted, he started on his stall tactics. His main one was, "They're on their way. But they're stuck in traffic."

I was new at this. This was my first time doing anything like this. I had no idea how the "game" was played.

And I'll tell you something. It was probably a good thing that I had no idea what I was doing.

Why do I say that? Because me not knowing what I was doing probably took the stress level of the situation down one notch with the Police.

Had I actually known what I was doing, knowing that the negotiator was just stringing me along, the situation could've turned out a lot worse.

There we were talking, the negotiator and I. I was asking for Lois and the FBI. And he was asking for one hostage at a time.

He was using his stall technique like a pro. He had me hook, line, and sinker. And he knew it.

Our "negotiations" went on for about two hours. I never got Lois or an FBI agent. He eventually got all six of the hostages.

One thing about that day. Over the course of that standoff, I'm sure at least one of the police officers who were around the bank had an opportunity to take me out. It was only by the grace of God, only by his divine protection, that no one got physically hurt or killed that day at the bank.

After I let my last hostage go, the standoff was over. I walked out of the bank and surrendered to the police. They took me to the Lee County Jail in Fort Myers, Florida.

Once they got me to the jail and they processed me, they put me in the suicide observation cell.

My death wish didn't leave me just because my bank plan failed. I was still just as confused, just as hopeless, just as obsessed with death as I was when I woke up that morning.

They booked me into jail on five counts of false imprisonment and one count of aggravated assault with a deadly weapon. They put my bail at $100,000.

I was in jail. And this time, I wasn't getting out any time soon. I was guilty, and everybody knew it.

I put six innocent people through mental, emotional torture they had no business going through.

I'm not excusing or justifying my actions that day.

I was wrong! I'm sorry for hurting all six of you.

However, with the mind frame that I was in back then, I didn't care about anybody, including myself.

My bank plan didn't turn out the way I hoped it would. However, it turned out the way God wanted it to. No one got physically hurt or killed. Back then, it was a loss in my eyes. But a win in God's eyes.

There I was, in the Lee County Jail in Fort Myers, Florida. After two or three weeks in the suicide observation cell, they decided to move me to the general population.

Eventually, I started to see my public defenders.

We started to come up with a trial strategy. They thought it would be in my best interest if we went for the insanity defense.

I had no idea about the legal system and about how it worked. This was my first time dealing with it. My thought was, "They're the professionals. Surely, they know what they're doing." I was wrong. I went with whatever they suggested. I was ignorant. I didn't know any better.

During one of our early visits, they told me that a trial date was set. And the date was nine months away—nine months away!

The longest time I spent in any psych hospital at any one time was at most five months. And they're telling me that my trial was nine months away.

And I was guilty. Which meant I was going to do time in prison. That didn't go over well with me. However, I had no one to blame but me. I brought this on myself.

So there I was in jail, just passing the time watching TV, playing cards, and reading. I wasn't doing anything to help in my defense. That was up to my public defenders, the professionals. I was wrong again.

Since we were going for the insanity defense, I had to talk to a psychiatrist. When it came time for me to talk with them, I knew him. He was one of the doctors I talked to when I was in one of the psych hospitals in Fort Myers.

So we were talking, and he was asking me all kinds of questions about the day in the bank. Asking questions about my past and other things. I don't remember getting any kind of an answer to what he was thinking.

My time in jail was passing with no major incidents. I kept doing what I was doing, watching TV, playing cards, and reading.

In the process of time, my trial date finally arrived. It was a two-day trial—from February 28, 2002, until March 1, 2002.

My public defenders thought it would be a good idea if I wore my orange jail jumpsuit during the trial. (They're the professionals, not me.)

My trial was on the move. Witness after witness was taking the stand, telling their version of what happened that day in the bank. Everyone in the courtroom knew I was guilty. I never denied that I wasn't.

Then they started calling the psychiatrists to the stand. Was I or was I not insane when I walked into that bank on May 9, 2001?

I believe they all thought there was something wrong with me. But I don't think any of them thought that I was insane according to the law.

Now both sides rested. The jury goes into deliberate. After forty-five minutes, they came back with a deadlock decision.

What does my public defender do? He sent them back in to deliberate some more.

The next time the jury came out, they were in agreement this time. They all found me guilty (which wasn't a surprise). But they didn't think I was insane at the time.

The trial was over. I was going to prison (again, not a surprise). Now it was up to the judge on how much time I would spend in prison.

When the sentencing day came, I stood in front of the judge. He said I was a danger to myself and to other people. I couldn't argue with him on that statement.

On all six counts against me, he sentenced me to six five-year sentences running consecutively for a total of thirty years.

My public defender asked the judge if I could get jail time credit. The judge said that I could. He took fourteen months off each of the six sentences. So instead of thirty years, I would only have to do twenty-three years.

But like I said before, I have no one to blame but myself. I did the crime. No one put a gun to my head. No one forced me to do it. I chose to do wrong. I deserved the time.

Now it's a waiting game. I have to wait for my name to be called to go to a reception center to be processed into prison. There's no telling how long it will take. I just have to wait my turn.

Eventually, my day to go to prison arrives. They sent me to the Orlando Reception Center in Orlando, Florida.

There's a lot more to being processed into prison than I thought there was.

It starts with being stripped searched. Then it moves on to your property being searched. The Officer tells us what we can and cannot keep. Then, it moves on to a physical, including any shots that we might need. Then it moves on to a group talk with one of the officers there. The officer is talking to us about the dos and don'ts of prison life, talking to us about what we can expect when we get there.

All this is done on the first day. After that, over the next few weeks, I talked with various other people: doctors, counselors, etc. They were determining if I had any physical problems, such as seizures, heart problems, aids, and cancer or if I had any mental health issues or if I had any special skills, such as electrician, construction, law experience, or welding. They were determining which prison they were going to send me to.

After I got done talking to everybody that I needed to talk to, it was just a matter of sitting back and waiting.

After about six weeks at Orlando Reception Center, I was on the move. They were sending me to Sumter Correctional Institution. I was at Sumter from September 15, 2002, until January 3, 2003.

I'll tell you something. God was looking out for me when he sent me to Sumter. That was the perfect first prison for me to go to. It was laid back and easygoing as far as prisons go.

As good as Sumter was, there was one major problem that I had with it. It was called the kitchen.

When I got to Sumter, they assigned me to work in the kitchen. Everyone who works in the kitchen works all three meals—breakfast, lunch, and dinner—five days a week. I lasted between two and three months doing this.

Remember, I'm brand-new to the system. I don't know how anything works. I didn't know that after one year, I could change jobs and put in for another one. I thought I was stuck in the kitchen for the next twenty years. I couldn't see myself doing that. So one morning, in the kitchen, my mind just had a nervous breakdown.

The officers came and took me to the observation cell. They kept me in there for a couple of days while they looked for a place to send me.

Just because I was in prison, it didn't take away the confusion, hopelessness, and desire for death that I still had.

And now add in a nervous breakdown. They were looking for a CSU within the Florida prison system that would take me.

They eventually found one. On January 3, 2003, Sumter transferred me to Charlotte Correctional Institution. I was in Charlotte from January 3, 2003, until January 30, 2003.

I haven't been in the prison system very long, but one thing I did hear about. I heard that Charlotte Correction Institution was a violent place.

So during the trip from Sumter to Charlotte, I was kind of nervous about what might happen when I got there. I didn't know what to expect. I didn't know if anyone was going to do anything to me or not.

But God had me covered. He had his protection over me. He kept everyone from doing anything to me.

At that time in my life, I didn't know God. I didn't want God. I wanted nothing to do with him. I was in my own lonely, dark world of death and despair.

But God still loved and protected me. He was still with me in spite of me.

When I got to the CSU in Charlotte, there was a nurse working there that I remembered. She worked as a nurse at G. Pierce Wood in Arcadia, Florida. That was one of the Florida psych hospitals that I was in.

It was nice to see a friendly face that I knew.

A few weeks after I got to the CSU, the doctor thought I was well enough to move from the CSU to the main compound in Charlotte.

After another week or two, Charlotte found me the next prison I was going to. They were transferring me to Tomoka Correctional Institution. I was at Tomoka from February 6, 2003, until November 20, 2006.

Tomoka was an average Florida prison as far as violence went. If you were looking for violence, it had no problem finding you. If you weren't looking for it, for the most part, it left you alone.

There is one major unwritten rule in prison. If anyone abides by this rule, their chances of avoiding violence and going home increase dramatically.

One major unwritten rule is this. You see, but you don't see. You hear, but you don't hear. If you see something, you don't see it. If you hear something, you don't hear it. What that means is "Mind your own business."

Let me give you an example of what I mean. You get sentenced to a five-year prison sentence. And you're just starting your time. You see another prisoner that's fifteen years into a life sentence with no parole doing drugs or robbing someone or whatever. You tell an officer what you saw. That prisoner goes to confinement because of you.

What value do you think that prisoner is going to put on your life? Your life means nothing to him now.

They're doing life anyway. They're going to die in prison. Whatever they do to you isn't going to affect them.

One thing about it. People in prison have a long memory toward other people who did wrong to them.

What you did in that situation is opened the door wide open for violence to come upon you.

Why? Because you didn't follow the unwritten rule. You didn't mind your own business.

Up to this point in my prison journey, I was still homicidal, suicidal, depressed, hopeless, with an "I don't care. What's the use" attitude.

However, that was about to change. God was about to turn my life around. He was about to bring me from death to life.

I believe God allowed me to have that nervous breakdown at Sumter just so he could get me to Tomoka. God wanted me at Tomoka at that time so he could spiritually save my life.

There I was at Tomoka Correctional Institution, just going through my day-to-day routine.

On September 29, 2003, I decided to go to the library. When I got there, I started looking through the section of the library dealing with death since that was still my main focus.

As I was searching the shelves for something to read, there it was. There was the book that God wanted me to read. Its title jumped at me like a flashing neon sign screaming, "Read me! Read me!"

The name of the book was called *To Hell and Back*. It's a book written by a cardiologist. It's a book about near-death experiences: people dying and coming back.

God was about to use this book to save my life.

I know when I mention near-death experience. People are dying and coming back. Some people will be skeptical if that really happens while other people will flat-out deny that there is such a thing.

The book has experiences from different people from all over the world. There were men and women. They were of different ages. Some were young. Others were middle-aged while others were older adults.

They were from all different religions: some Christians, some Muslims, some atheists, etc.

Some saw the beauty and splendor of heaven while others saw the terrors of hell.

God used this book to show me that hell was not where he wanted me to be.

I wasn't even halfway through the book. The next day, September 30, 2003, I was in Chaplain Perry Davis's office, surrendering my life to Jesus Christ.

When I mention the topic of heaven and hell, people have their own different opinions. Some believe there is a heaven and hell. Some don't believe there is such a place while other people aren't sure or don't care.

But I'm pretty sure we can all agree on one thing. When we take our last breath on this earth, we're all going to know what the truth is, whether there actually is a heaven and hell or not.

Let me ask those people who don't believe there's a heaven and hell or who aren't sure about it one question. Are you willing to bet your souls that you're right? That's going to be a long time to suffer if you're wrong.

There I was, at Tomoka Correctional Institution, a brand-new person. I was now saved. I was now a child of God.

And the first major area of my life that Jesus healed me of was my homicidal and suicidal thoughts. My obsession with death was gone.

What those psych hospitals, doctors, and medications couldn't do, Jesus did!

Before Jesus delivered me from those evil spirits, I was like a modern-day Legion—Legion from the book of Mark chapter 5. Chains couldn't keep him, and he roamed among the tombs.

I was a modem-day Legion. My chains were psych hospitals. They couldn't hold me. I was in and out of a dozen hospitals that couldn't help me in any way, shape, or form.

I roamed among the tombs. I couldn't get away from the thought of death. I was consumed by it.

But Jesus delivered me from the chains of psych hospitals. And he delivered me from the tombs of death that was consuming me.

He sat me down. He clothed me. He put me in my right mind. It was nothing I did. It was everything he did!

God was working on me. He was pruning, refining, and purifying me to become the man of God that he needed me to be.

But I was only giving him a half-hearted effort at best. I had a lot of faults, flaws, and issues that I wasn't even trying to deal with.

I was one of those Christians that knew I was saved. I was reading the Word. I was going to church services. I was going to Bible studies.

But I was lazy in a lot of areas that I had no business being lazy in. Areas such as praying, fasting, witnessing, and crucifying my flesh.

I was feeding my flesh as much or more than I was feeding my spirit. I wasted a lot of years in this spiritual condition. I have no one to blame but myself.

Well, my time at Tomoka Correctional Institution was moving along. I was going through my day-to-day routine.

Over time, I was about to be on the move again. Tomoka was about to transfer me. They were sending me to Everglades Correctional Institution. I was at Everglades from December 1, 2006, until March 30, 2007.

When I got to Everglades, my classification officer asked me if I wanted to go to another prison that had a lot of different classes.

If I could better myself, why not? So I told him, "Yes. I'd go."

Four months later, Everglades was transferring me to Wakulla Correctional Institution. I was at Wakulla from April 3, 2007, until September 16, 2008.

However, it would be less than two years later, and I would be right back at Everglades. I would be back there due to circumstances beyond my control.

So I got to Wakulla and found out that there were a lot of classes that we could take there.

If someone in the Florida Department of Corrections wanted to better themselves in an educational aspect, then Wakulla was the place for them to go.

Once I got settled in, I started getting into some of the classes they were offering.

A few of the classes that I completed were the computer class, accounting 101, and time management.

I also joined the gavel club. That's a place where you learn how to become a better public speaker. I gave four speeches. But I never really felt comfortable speaking in front of crowds.

I also took a class called small business concepts. It was a class that taught us how to start and run a small business.

Have you ever had an idea that could help a lot of people? And your idea would fade into the background of your thoughts. But every once in a while, it would come to the front of your mind as strong as ever.

Well, that's what happened to me in this small business class. The idea that I had twenty-plus years ago about running around the country came to the front of my mind. However, it was going to be for a different cause.

The run around the country was going to be the same. But this time, the cause was going to be for homeless and abused children.

I was taking this business class to start a shelter for homeless and abused children. The shelter was going to be called the Spark of Hope Children's Shelter.

The class taught us how to write up a business plan, including the floor plan for our business.

However, over the course of time and varying circumstances, I got rid of the business plan for the shelter. But I still remember most of it in my head, including the floor plan.

While I was at Wakulla, a major negative situation happened to me. This was the only time that it happened during my entire prison sentence. It was no one's fault. It was beyond everybody's control.

It was sometime in July 2008. I was still occasionally distance running. It was July in Florida, which meant it was hot. I'm well into my run, just past the six-mile mark.

When, out of nowhere, they call me to the captain's office for a pee test.

As you can imagine, after running six miles in the July heat, I was sweating pretty good.

I got to the captain's office, and I couldn't go right away.

They gave me plenty of water and two hours to produce a urine sample. My body wasn't cooperating.

After two hours and no sample, they had no choice but to lock me up to send me to confinement.

That's why I said it was no one's fault. They were asking for something that my bladder wasn't ready to give them.

They had a job to do. They didn't know if I was clean or dirty. I couldn't blame them for doing their job.

Off to confinement I went. I stayed in there for the next fifty days. And they took away thirty days of my gain time.

Fifty days after I couldn't pee for them, I'm on the move again. Wakulla was transferring me back to Everglades. Everglades round two. This time, I was there from September 26, 2008, until April 29, 2011.

Everglades was an average prison. So it didn't take long to get into a daily routine. Prison life is all about routine. You have to keep yourself busy. That's how your time moves quickly.

One major positive event happened to me while I was at Everglades. I became a college graduate!

The chapel at Everglades offered an AA degree and a BA degree in biblical studies. To get the AA degree, you had to complete twelve courses. To get the BA degree, you had to complete sixteen courses. Each course had an average of four to five lessons in each one.

The class met once a week at the chapel. We'd discuss scripture. Anyone who had their homework done could turn it in at that time.

One thing about that class. You could take as long as you wanted to get your degree. You could go fast, or you could go slow. The pace was up to you.

For me, personally, it took me one year to get my AA degree. I started in October 2008 and finished in October 2009.

I was doing something positive and productive with my time in prison.

During my time in prison, I've seen a lot of different people with a lot of different personalities.

Some of them were good. Some were bad. Some of them were predators, preying on the weak, preying on the simple, preying on the new people. They had the "game" down to a science.

Some were prey. Clueless as to what was going on. They were caught in the trap of the predator's game.

I've also seen people in prison. It was their first time in. They were there because they made one momentary bad decision like I did. They knew that prison wasn't for them. Prison for them was about to become an eye-opening once in a lifetime. I learned my lesson and never again experienced it.

On the other hand, I've also seen people in prison who have no intention of changing their behavior.

They have no problem with the prison life. They have three hots and a cot with absolutely no responsibilities. They get three hot meals a day and a bed to lie down on every night. They're doing life on the installment plan, and it doesn't bother them at all.

Prison is all about what you personally make it. If you want to better yourself, you can do that. If you want to get sucked into the depravity of the prison life, you can do that as well.

But whatever choice you make, you're responsible for it. You can't blame anyone else for the choice you make.

My time at Everglades was moving along pretty good. My time there was coming to a close. I was about to be on the move again.

The next prison on my Florida prison tour was Graceville Correctional Institution. I was at Graceville from May 3, 2011, until July 12, 2013.

I personally didn't like being at Graceville for one main reason: drugs!

The compound was flooded with drugs, mainly K-2. You couldn't get away from it. Everywhere you went, you smelled it.

That stuff was dangerous and deadly. I remember seeing a guy in the dorm that I was in smoking some K-2. He went nuts. He went into his cell, closed the door, and started hollering really loud.

It didn't take long before five or six officers came into the dorm. They went to his cell, opened the door, cuffed him, and escorted him out of the dorm.

The officers couldn't stop the K-2 from coming onto the compound. They didn't try to stop it. They just dealt with it as each situation arose.

During my prison sentence, my mom would visit me when she could. During one of our visits to Graceville, she told me it was time to get me out of prison.

How and when that thought came to her, I have no idea. But it definitely sounded like a good idea to me.

Somehow, someway, the idea of clemency was formed. We were going to ask the governor's board for a reduction of my sentence.

Mom got busy on the outside. She was getting all the papers she wanted and needed together that were going to the governor's board.

I worked on my end to get all the paperwork I needed. All the proper forms and documents together.

Eventually, we both got all our paperwork together. Somewhere around late 2011 or early

2012, we sent everything we had to the governor's board. Now all we could do was wait.

Over time, I was on the transfer bus again. My next stop was Walton Correctional Institution. I was at Walton from July 15, 2013, until May 22, 2017.

What can I say about Walton? It was an average prison. If you were looking for violence, it wasn't hard to find. If you weren't looking for it, for the most part, it avoided you.

There were two major situations that happened to me while I was at Walton—one bad and one good.

The bad situation that happened was my brother's death.

My brother Jeff visited me a few times while I was at Walton. I already knew that he was suicidal. And then seeing him face to face, seeing how he was, hearing what he was saying. I could see the signs in him—the depression, the regret, the hurt, and the pain that was inside him.

I witnessed to him on one of our last visits. I told him what Jesus could do for him. Jeff already saw the change that Jesus did in me. I told him that Jesus could do the same thing for him that he did with me. But he didn't receive it at that time.

It wasn't long after that, and I was called to the chaplain's office. Very seldom is it a good thing when a prisoner is called to the chaplain's office. And seeing and hearing Jeff in the condition he was in, I wasn't surprised when I got the news that he killed himself.

When I got to the chaplain's office, Mom told me over the phone what happened, how he did it, and when he did it.

Obviously, she was crying. I was trying my best to comfort her. I was reminding her that Jeff was finally out of his physical and emotional pain. But those words were doing very little, if anything, to comfort her.

The chaplain allowed Mom and I to talk for a few minutes.

After Mom and I finished talking, the chaplain and the captain talked to me for a few minutes. They were seeing how I was. If I was okay or if I needed help. I was okay.

As the captain was walking me out of the chapel, he asked me if I believed in prayer. I said that I did.

At Walton, they have a program called the reentry program. This captain walked me right into the reentry class as it was going on. The officer who was running the program had everyone who wanted to in the class pray for my family and me.

After that, I went back to the dorm. I don't remember what I did for the rest of that day.

However, the next day, I was called to the reentry program. I was asked to sit in one of the classes with them.

During the class, I was brought in to be interviewed for the program. They told me about the class, about the dorm, and about the rules.

I explained to them that I wasn't ready to get into the actual reentry class.

So they told me that I could be a full-time houseman in the reentry dorm. I agreed to that. By the end of that week, I was moved into the reentry dorm.

What can I say about the reentry dorm? The average prisoner on the compound was not going to make it very long in that dorm. Why? Because Mr. Smith, the officer who was over the program, ran a tight ship.

He had rules for the dorm over and above the compound rules. Rules such as your locker had to be up off the floor by either 5:30 or 6:00 a.m. You couldn't walk in between the bunks without permission. There was no talking in the dayroom when a television show or movie was on. When a commercial was on, you could talk. When the show came back on, you had to stop talking. No yelling or loud talking in the dorm at any time. These were just some of the rules for the dorm.

The reentry class was a six-month class. At the end of six months, they had a graduation ceremony for everyone who had completed the class.

There I was in the dorm, doing my houseman duties. And something strange was happening. The dorm was starting to grow on me. I was starting to fit in. I was starting to make a few friends.

Over the course of a few months, I decided that I would like to give the reentry class a try. So when they started the next class, I signed up for it.

There wasn't really anything hard about the class. For the most part, it was all about getting us to think—to think about our past, to think about what brought us to prison, to think about our lives, and to think about how we can change for the better, now and in the future. The class gave us tools to help us to change.

When I started the reentry class, Mr. Smith started a brand-new class. A brand-new class that was separate from the reentry class. It was a six-month class designed to teach one thing—leadership! The class was designed to teach the participants how to become better, more effective leaders.

There I was in the reentry class, doing everything I was supposed to do. And in the dorm, I followed the rules as best I could.

Over the course of time, another reentry graduation was here. I completed all the work that needed to be completed in order to graduate.

The first leadership class was about to graduate with the reentry class.

To be selected to be in the leadership class, the first requirement is graduating from the reentry class. Other requirements included following the dorm rules and leading by example, and they had to see leadership potential in you.

The people who chose who did and didn't get into the leadership class thought that I met all the qualifications. They chose me to be in the second leadership class.

It was a good class. It taught us the do's and don'ts of being a good leader.

As good as the class was, I had one major problem. Me! At that point in my life, I didn't have the boldness and confidence in myself to be a good, effective leader.

My mind was still trapped in the past. I was still thin-skinned. I was still concerned about what people were thinking about me, saying about me, and going to do to me.

You can't have the mind frame I had and be a good, effective leader.

While I was at Walton Correctional Institution, I received two letters from the governor's board concerning my clemency.

The first one was somewhere around 2014. It was a letter informing me that the governor's board sent a letter to the director of Clemency Investigations requesting them to investigate my case. Why would they request them to do this? To make their recommendation as to whether or not they think I should get my reduction of sentence or not.

The second letter I received from the governor's board was somewhere around 2016. It was a letter informing me of the director of Clemency Investigations' recommendation. Their recommendation was no reduction of sentences.

I have no idea why they recommended turning me down. I was disappointed. I didn't understand why they would turn me down.

That would turn out to be the last letter I got concerning my clemency. What a letdown.

While I was at Walton, I tried to get to their work camp. In order for me to get to the work camp, I needed to get a doctor's approval.

So Walton sent me to Lake Butler Medical Center.

I was at Lake Butler from February 17, 2015, until May 21, 2015.

As I was waiting to see the doctor, I was still occasionally distance running.

One day, I decided to run on the track they had at Lake Butler. During the run, one of my calves gave out on me. It said, "No more."

That run was the beginning of the end for my distance running.

My running days were over. How do I know that for sure? Because every time I started running after that, it didn't take long before one or the other calf started to flare up. They were telling me, "We're not going to do this. Your running is done."

I eventually saw the doctor at Lake Butler. They checked me out and gave me a clean bill of health. I was cleared by the doctor to go to the work camp at Walton.

However, when I got back to Walton Correctional Institution, for whatever unknown reason they had, they wouldn't let me go to their work camp.

Even though I couldn't go to their work camp, God still used my time at Walton for his glory and for my good. He got me into the reentry class and the leadership class.

I was five months into the leadership class with one month to go until graduation. I wouldn't make it to graduation.

I was about to be on the transfer bus again. Walton was transferring me to Cross City Correctional Institution.

When I got to Cross City, they sent me to the work camp. I was at Cross City work camp from June 12, 2017, until December 18, 2017.

The work camp was a change that I wasn't prepared for. I was used to living with 144 guys or more per dorm. When I got to the work camp, there were 70 guys per dorm. It was a lot smaller than I was used to. It was a refreshing change.

After I got settled into the work camp, they gave me a job. They put me on the inside grounds. All I did was pick up trash on the compound with 10 to 15 other guys.

They had me do that for two to three weeks. After that, they gave me my gate pass. What did that mean? It meant I could work outside the gate.

Do you know how excited I was about this opportunity! After many years of being locked up behind the fence, now I'm working outside the gate.

At first, they kept me around the work camp. Cutting the grass and picking up trash.

They were understandably testing me. They were seeing if I was going to run or not.

Over the course of a couple of weeks, I showed them that I was going to be good and not run.

So one day, they took me into town to work. I remember that day. I was with a work crew that was putting tree branches into a wood chipper.

As we were working, a guy on a bicycle rode past us. His riding past us gave me a hunger for freedom, a hunger to get out of prison that I never felt before. But God wasn't ready for me to get out yet.

Over the next two months or so, they had me working around the compound three or four days a week. And out in the community one or two days a week.

Over time, as I was showing them that I was actually going to work, it started to change. It started to become two or three days around the compound and two or three days out in the community.

Eventually, I worked my way permanently into the community.

At Cross City, there were five five-man squads that worked in the community four days a week. One squad did strictly painting. One squad did strictly concrete. One squad did strictly tree branches and overhangs, putting them into the chipper. And the other two squads were miscellaneous. Doing everything from cutting grass and weed eating to picking up trash to cleaning out storm drains.

I was on one of the miscellaneous squads. One thing about it was we worked hard, and we stayed busy.

One day, as I was in the dorm, I heard another guy tell someone else about another prison that sounded pretty good. It was a prison where you could wear street clothes.

Well, that sounded good to me. I would be wearing street clothes. I would be wearing what I wanted to wear (within reason). Not the prison clothes that I've been wearing. Feeling at least a little free, at least mentally.

I told my mom about it. She made some phone calls. Somehow, she found the place (so we thought). They put me on the list to go.

Within four weeks of being put on the list, I was on the move again. Cross City work camp transferred me to Gadsden Reentry Center. I was at Gadsden from December 27, 2017, until May 26, 2020.

Any hope and any good thoughts that I may have had about Gadsden Reentry Center were quickly and utterly smashed to pieces. Within the first week of being there, I was already tired of that place.

As far as us being able to wear street clothes there, that was a definite no.

The woman that Mom talked to about Gadsden either lied or had no idea what she was talking about.

Gadsden was the worst prison that I was in. It was my own living hell.

I've been in psych hospitals that were run better than Gadsden. In a lot of the psych hospitals that I've been in, the patients in the hospitals were a lot more respectful than some of the prisoners were at Gadsden.

While I was at Gadsden, it was an emotional and mental battle. Even though I was a Christian, there were more than a few times that I wanted to hurt some of the people there physically.

It was only Jesus himself that kept me from physically hurting anyone.

I wanted to hurt them strictly because of one thing: disrespect. Let me give a few examples of their disrespect—full-scale debates about useless topics across the dorm after lights-out. The television is up as loud as it can go, and you can't hear it because people are debating and arguing in the dayroom. Certain people slammed dominos on the dayroom table every time they played just because they could. When a football game was on, it didn't matter if it was an afternoon or an evening game.

Certain people were screaming and yelling at every play like they were at the game.

While I was at Gadsden, they assigned me to work in the kitchen on the morning shift. The morning shift got up at 2:30 a.m. and was out the door by 3:00 a.m.

With all the disrespect that was going on daily and the officers doing nothing about it, it was hard to get any sleep in that place.

I eventually had enough. I wrote a request to the head classification officer requesting a job change. I asked them to get me out of the kitchen.

I told the Lord that if he didn't change my job by a certain date, I was going to hurt myself. I was getting out of the kitchen one way or another.

It was no more than two days later, and I got my job change. They took me out of the kitchen and put me as a houseman.

There were two things that kept me from going stupid at Gadsden Reentry Center.

The first one was Jesus. A lot of people there knew I was a Christian. So it was his name, his reputation on the line.

Had I gone off and got stupid, I would've disgraced and dishonored Jesus. I would've blown my witness for him. I would've given Satan a win that he had no business getting. And I would've given Jesus a loss that he had no business getting.

The second reason was this. I was trying to get out of prison. I wasn't trying to back up my time.

If I would've gone off and got stupid, I would've, at the least, gone to confinement. I would've lost more gain time, which would mean more time in prison.

I was trying to avoid both situations like the plague.

One good thing happened while I was at Gadsden. I became eligible for work release.

In the Florida Prison System, anyone with eighteen months or less remaining on their sentence is eligible to go to work release.

Work Release is a center where you actually wear street clothes. You wear street clothes because in order to be at a work release center, you have to get a legitimate paying job in the community.

So when I signed up for work release at Gadsden, that gave me even more motivation not to get stupid.

At this point, let me take a minute to talk to all the people who think prison is easy. They think it's a country club.

First off, let me say that I respect your right to your opinion and to your point of view.

With that being said, I respectfully have to disagree with you. I respectfully have to say that you have no idea what you're talking about.

Unless you've been in a state prison for five straight years or more, you can't possibly understand how mentally difficult it actually is.

Being in prison physically isn't really that difficult as long as you follow the unwritten rule.

On the other hand, mentally and emotionally, it's torture. We are being told what to do and when to do it. The stress of violence happens at any time. I am putting up with disrespectful people twenty-four hours a day, seven days a week, and having no privacy.

Don't get me wrong. Ninety-seven percent of the prison population broke the law in some way to land up in prison. They deserve to be there like I did.

However, to think that doing time in state prison is easy is like "club med" is a total lie.

How would you handle a situation like that?

Could you handle a situation like that? Being in a state prison for five-plus straight years.

So there I was at Gadsden. Holding my tongue, I was not going stupid, waiting to go to work release.

One morning, as I was doing my houseman duties, my name was called, along with fifteen to twenty other guys. It was our day to go to work release.

When I signed up for work release, she asked me for two choices of where I wanted to go. My two choices were Pensacola and Tallahassee. They approved me to go to Pensacola.

I was on my way to Pensacola's work release. There were around ten other guys that went to Pensacola with me that day. I was at Pensacola work release from May 26, 2020, until September 14, 2020.

Work release was a transition for me. It helped me go from a prison mentality to actually interacting with society again.

I had to get re-adjusted to society's ways. The things that society takes for granted, I had to re-learn—things such as doing my own laundry. I haven't done my own laundry in twenty years. That was something I had to relearn.

We were allowed to have our own cell phones at work release. A cell phone is something I never had in my life. I've never seen one. I've never held one. And I've certainly never used one. Learning how to use a cell phone was something I was going to have to learn from scratch.

I eventually got a job working at McDonald's. After almost twenty years, I was actually getting paid money to work. It felt good.

I was interacting with society and interacting with my bosses and coworkers at work. It was weird at first because it's been so long since I did that. But it didn't take long before it started to feel normal again.

Mom and Roger, my stepdad, bought me everything I needed for work release. They bought me clothes, my cell phone, pillows, sheets, blankets, toiletries, etc. And they drove it over from DeFuniak Springs to Pensacola. That's a pretty far drive.

I wouldn't have made it through my life before prison, during prison, and after prison without Jesus and without my family.

Jesus and family support are so vitally important to getting through this life, especially for those people who are locked up.

I put my family through so much shame, stress, and confusion. But yet they're still behind me. They're still willing to help me when I need help. They're willing to go out of their way, driving from DeFuniak Springs to Pensacola for me.

I don't deserve my family. But I'm certainly glad and thankful that they're still behind me.

After I'd been at work release for a few months, getting into my daily routine, getting into my work routine, a hurricane was about to throw a wrench into the mix.

What happened was this. We all knew the hurricane was coming. And this particular storm was going to dump a lot of water, which meant that places were going to flood, including the Pensacola work release center.

So the warden for the work release center and whoever else was involved thought it would be safest for us if they relocated us to another place.

They decided to send us to Century Work Camp.

I remember the day before we moved. We were told to pack all our possessions into garbage bags. Then we brought all our possessions into a secure room at the center. We put our possessions in the chairs and tops of school desks.

The room where our possessions were flooded from the hurricane. A lot of our stuff got wet and/or ruined.

The next day was moving day. They loaded us onto either one or two buses. And off to Century Work Camp we went.

That would turn out to be the last time I saw Pensacola's work release center.

We eventually made it to Century Work Camp. I believe the original plan was for us to stay there just a couple of days and then go back to Pensacola. It didn't turn out that way.

I didn't know it at the time. But I was about to leave prison from Century Work Camp. I was there from September 14, 2020, until November 15, 2020.

When we got to Century, they stripped, searched us, gave us our toiletries, and headed us to our dorm.

Since this was happening during COVID-19, they quarantined us for either seven or fourteen days. We couldn't go anywhere. They brought three meals a day to us.

The reason we were at Century for an extended period of time was because when the hurricane did hit, the work release got flooded. They had to do a lot of repairs to the work release center that they weren't expecting to do.

While we were at Century, after our quarantine was over, they still kept us separate from the rest of the compound.

However, they let us go to the canteen. They let us go to the recreation field. And they gave us movies to watch in the dorm.

Over the course of time, they brought all our property from the work release center to the work camp.

We all had an opportunity to go through all our property to see what was wet or ruined. We also went through our stuff because the staff was allowing us to bring certain things back to the dorm with us. Things such as books, radios, and certain other things that I can't remember right now.

When they allowed us to bring back some of our stuff, that definitely calmed the dorm down.

My time at Century Work Camp and in the Florida Department of Corrections was getting shorter and shorter. Day by day, my time was coming to an end.

I came into prison serving Satan. I was leaving prison serving Jesus!

Have I been a "perfect" Christian in prison since my conversion? Absolutely not! Have I said things that I had no business saying? Yes. Have I gotten in the flesh more times than I should have? Yes. Have I done things that I had no business doing? Yes.

I'm not perfect. I'm still a fleshly human being. I have faults, flaws, and issues that still need to be dealt with. I'm a child of God, and that's a work in progress.

I've messed up. I've disgraced my Lord Jesus.

I've given Satan wins and Jesus losses that neither deserved.

On the other hand, I've also glorified Jesus by encouraging and edifying the brothers. By conducting Bible studies. By planting and watering seeds.

In short, I'm a human being that's a Christian who's a work in progress!

What does the next stage of my life have in store for me? I have no idea. But two things I do know. First, God is with me. I'm not doing the rest of my life alone. And two. I'm absolutely ready to leave prison.

CHAPTER 5

Free Man Again?

EOS Day! Nineteen years, six months, six days after walking into that Fort Myers, Florida bank, I was walking out of prison at Century Correctional Institution.

I'll tell you something. It felt weird that first week out of prison. I was not being told what to do or when to do it—being able to do what I wanted, when I wanted, and how I wanted. That took a little getting used to.

Mom and Roger agreed to pick me up at Century and take me home. On the way home, we stopped at Golden Corral for lunch.

Again, all I can say is it was a weird feeling. I saw all the customers moving around, eating, and filling their plates. It was business as usual for them.

This was the first time in almost twenty years that I could eat what I wanted to eat and take more than ten minutes to do it. Lunch was very good. It was delicious. I definitely eat my fill.

Eventually, we made it back to DeFuniak Springs. I saw their fifth wheel for the first time. It was bigger and nicer than I expected it to be.

They allowed me to stay with them until I got my own trailer. It took about a month for me to get situated before I got my own trailer.

There were a few things that needed to be dealt with before getting my own place. I needed to go through all the papers that Mom saved from my incarceration. I needed to go through all the clothes that I inherited from my brother. The 2006 Jeep Commander that I inherited from my brother was being worked on as well.

Most of the clothes that I got from Jeff fit nicely. And the winter clothes he had come in real handy.

By mid to late December 2020, it happened. I got my own trailer. It was a brand-new, twenty-foot Coleman pull behind. It had everything I needed: a bed, shower, microwave, refrigerator, etc. The most important thing it came with was quietness and privacy.

Mom and Roger helped me get everything I needed for it. Roger showed how to hook everything up; the sewer hose, electricity, water line, and the hitch. None of that stuff is too hard. It doesn't take long to catch on.

I had everything I needed to start my post-prison life. I had my own trailer. I had all the clothes I needed. I had my own transportation, the Jeep Commander. And I had my family helping me.

You would think that I would be overwhelmed with joy being in the position I was in right now. And, in all reality, I should've been.

But I wasn't. When I walked out of prison, I didn't feel any euphoric, walking on cloud nine feeling.

Don't get me wrong. It was good. It was nice. I definitely learned my lesson. But I didn't get any special feelings.

It was just another day. The only difference was I was out of prison, not still in there.

The thing about it is this. Even though I was spiritually free and physically free, I was still emotionally in bondage.

I was still allowing my past to have control over me. I still cared about what people thought of me, said about me, and did to me. I never got myself out of that prison I was in.

I was trying to be a people pleaser instead of a God pleaser. I was trying to please people so that they'd like me. I was trying to fit in somewhere. I was trying to be accepted by people.

But that's just it. We're never going to fit in with society. We're never going to be accepted by them.

The people we fit in with are God's people. The people that are going to accept us are God's people. The only person we are to please is God himself.

We have to realize who we are and who we belong to. We are children of God, his sons and daughters. And he accepts us as his children through Jesus Christ.

The problem was that I was focused on the physical part of my life, not the spiritual part. And that had me out of focus.

What I was doing was this. I was expecting the world to do what only God can do. I was expecting the things of the world, especially my jobs, to give me happiness, to give me purpose, which it can never do.

I was chasing the wind, trying to find where I fit in, trying to find my place in life.

My heart was right. I was seeking God's guidance. I was seeking his direction. I would ask him to open doors that he wanted me to go through. And close doors that he didn't. However, every time he opened a door for me, I'd shut it because I allowed my flesh to talk me out of it.

Just like before prison, I was doing the same thing after prison. Going from state to state, job to job, trying to find fulfillment.

There we were, Roger, Mom, and me in Florida. Spring was coming up, which meant Mom and Roger's annual trip to Elkhart, Indiana.

They go up there to avoid the hurricanes.

This year, I was going with them. Off to Elkhart we went. It took us ten to fourteen days to get there. But eventually, we arrived.

It's an average city. Almost every city you go to, they're going to have the same things to do. They're going to have restaurants, bars, movie theaters, shops, malls, etc.

While we were there, I'd spend my days reading the word, watching television, going with Mom into town for this or that.

At night, I'd be over at their place eating dinner and watching television.

Summer was passing, and fall was on the way. Plans were being made. Mom and Roger were headed back to Florida.

I had different plans. My sister and I talked it over. She said it was okay if I stayed with her for a while.

Since she lives in a house and there was nowhere to park my trailer, I sold it.

A week or two before Mom and Roger headed back to Florida, I sold my trailer and headed to Michigan to live with my sister.

She has four cats and one big, red dog. It took a while before the cats started to warm up to me. But the dog and I got along right away.

After I got settled in, God found me a job at Joe's Produce in the deli department.

It was one of those doors that God opened. And I let my flesh slam it shut.

Living with my sister was good. We were getting along great. Everything was going smoothly.

Then came a snag. It was nothing she said or did.

It was me (as usual).

I started thinking about my life. I was fifty-seven years old, and I've never been out on my own.

All my life, I've had people helping me and taking care of me. I appreciate everyone that's helped me in my life.

The point is, I'm a grown adult man who's never lived on my own.

So one day, with Kim at work and it being my day off, I hit the road. It was time to see if I could or couldn't make it on my own.

I was on my way to Pittsburgh, Pennsylvania.

Why did I choose Pittsburgh? Two reasons. First, I have family there that I haven't seen since before I went to prison. Second, I wanted to visit the place where I grew up. I wanted to see the house and neighborhood where I lived. And I wanted to see the school where I graduated from.

My intention when I got to Pittsburgh was to stay there, get a job, get a place, and put down roots. It didn't happen.

I got to Pittsburgh just fine. I got a hotel room that I was paying for by the week.

The day after I got there, I visited the place where I grew up—the house, the neighborhood, and the school where I graduated. It changed a lot. So that was accomplished.

Now it was time to settle down, buckle down, and get my life started.

I was looking for apartments to stay at. A lot of them were asking for the first month's rent and security. A lot of them were doing background checks. And some had waiting lists.

It was taking too long to get a job. My money was running out. I was getting frustrated.

I was starting to think about thoughts that I had no business thinking about.

Remember, I was expecting the world to do only what God could do.

I was holding on to hope that things were going to change and start going my way.

And besides that, Christmas was coming up. I didn't want to do anything stupid during Christmas.

So my thought was if something didn't break my way after the beginning of the year, I was going to hurt myself.

I know that was the wrong thought to have. I know that was a fleshly, worldly thought. But I was looking back over my life and realized that I'd made one bad decision after another after another.

I was fifty-seven years old and had nothing to show for my life. No wife. No kids. No career. No nothing. It wasn't a good feeling. It was depressing.

I was a poster child for a wasted, unfruitful life.

Christmas was good that year. I spent Christmas with my Aunt, with my cousins, and with their families.

My cousin Dave had his Christmas dinner first. I got to meet his kids and their kids. They definitely take after Dave. They're all very enthusiastic and energetic. I have to say that Dave did a good job raising his kids.

Then a couple of days later, it was my cousin Bob's turn to cook Christmas dinner. I had an opportunity to meet his kids. They were more laid back and reserved. Bob also did a good job raising his kids.

I had a good time at both dinners. It was nice finally seeing both Bob and Dave's kids. I heard so much about them while I was in prison. Now, I got to see them in person.

Christmas is over. New Year's is over. The beginning of the new year is here. Are things finally going to go my way or not? Nope. It's not going to happen.

I was tired. I was fed up. I hated the way my life was going.

And why was I feeling this way? Because I was in the flesh, not the spirit. I was looking through physical eyes, not spiritual ones. I was expecting the world to do something that it could never do.

I cried out to God more than a few times, asking him to either help me out of this situation or take me home.

I was ready to die. I was mentally and emotionally beat up and exhausted. I didn't want to hurt myself. I just wanted relief.

I've been seeking answers for the past couple of weeks to the question of what is the meaning of life.

I'm not talking about the spiritual meaning of life. I'm talking about the physical meaning of life.

Think about it. We go to work, and we come home. We cut the grass. We work around the house.

We pay bills. We work on the car. Why? What's the use of doing these things? What do we get out of doing these things? It made no sense to me.

It was a Sunday morning. I was in my Pittsburgh hotel room. And I needed answers.

Then, an idea came into my head. Go somewhere totally different. Somewhere that I don't know anyone and no one knows me.

My choice was Bangor, Maine. What was in Bangor, Maine? I was hoping answers were there. There was no other reason to go there.

My idea was when I got to Bangor if I didn't get the answers I was looking for, I'd end it.

I was as confused as I've ever been. I haven't been this confused since my "psych" years.

So I packed everything up, put it in the Jeep, and headed for Bangor.

When I got to Bangor, did I get the answers I was looking for? Yes and then some.

God spoke to me loud and clear in my spirit and through a song.

First, the song—the song is called "Jesus Is Coming Back" by Jordan Feliz.

I know from scripture that Jesus is coming back for his church. I read it countless times.

Even though I read it in scripture, it never really sank in. The light never came on in my head. It never became real to me.

One day, as that song was playing on the radio, God opened my eyes! He made that scripture real to me. Jesus is coming back for his church. It's not a question of if. It's a question of when!

As he opened my eyes to that reality, he put in my spirit one word: witness!

The physical meaning of my life is the same as my spiritual meaning. Witness! Get people ready for the return of Jesus.

I've made a lot of bad decisions in my life, both as an unbeliever and as a Christian.

I've done things I shouldn't have. I've said things I shouldn't have. I've thought things I shouldn't have. I've hurt, shamed, embarrassed, and disgraced a lot of people. I've figuratively spit in people's faces. I've broken the trust of people. I've failed my family as a son, as a brother, and as a Christian.

But that's what this book is all about. It's my witness, my testimony for Jesus. I've been stuck on stupid more than my fair share of times.

In spite of everything I've done, Jesus still loved me. He still cared about me. He still saved me.

Think about this. Jesus loved me, cared about me, and saved me just like he loves you, cares about you, and wants to save you.

Are you tired of being on the bottom? Are you tired of the way your life is going? Are you tired of being in bondage to your addictions? Do you want to be free? Do you want peace in your life?

Jesus is the only one who can give you what you're looking for. He's the only one who can be everything you need him to be.

He's waiting with open arms to receive you. He's knocking on the door of people's hearts, waiting for them to let him in.

Will you receive him? Will you let him in?

ABOUT THE AUTHOR

Richard Bryson was born in Pittsburgh, Pennsylvania. He now lives in Brookings, South Dakota. Richard has never been married and has no children. He has an AA degree in biblical studies. Richard has a lifetime of experience in what not to do. He would love somehow to help troubled kids.

Milton Keynes UK
Ingram Content Group UK Ltd.
UKHW050934170424
441314UK00001B/44